# American Watercolor Painting

# American Watercolor Painting

BY DONELSON F. HOOPES

Galahad Books • New York City

First published in 1977 in New York by Watson-Guptill Publications, a division of Billboard Publications, Inc.,
1515 Broadway, New York, NY 10036

This edition published in the United States of America in 1981 by
Galahad Books
95 Madison Avenue
New York, New York 10016
By arrangement with Watson-Guptill Publications

Library of Congress Catalog Card Number: 81-81162
ISBN: 0-88365-561-6
Printed in the United States of America

# ACKNOWLEDGMENTS

The present survey of the development of water-color painting in America covers a period of about 150 years, beginning around 1800. Within the limitations imposed by the physical size of this single volume, this writer has attempted to deal fairly in his selection of the artists represented. There will be readers who will find, perhaps, their favorite artist missing from the roll call; that is inevitable. Both the selection of artists and the number of works assigned to each are matters that reflect on the author's judgment and preferences, and the whole is offered in admiration of the many and diverse talents who so magnificently adorn the history of American art.

In the preparation of this book, a number of individuals extended themselves to me in ways that warrant special thanks. To Dr. William H. Gerdts, The Graduate School, City University of New York; to Theodore E. Stebbins, Jr., Curator of American Paintings and Sculpture, Yale University Art Gallery; and to Lea Rosson, Assistant Curator, The University of Kansas Museum of Art, I am especially indebted for help in securing necessary, and sometimes elusive, permissions to reproduce from various private collectors. The Archives of American Art, with its indispensable resources of information, was consistently helpful; to the Director of the West Coast Area Office, Dr. Paul Karlstrom, my thanks and appreciation. To the many dealers, private collectors, and museum staff members to whom I addressed appeals for assistance in this project go my special — if collective — thanks. While space limitations preclude individual public acknowledgment, my gratitude is none the less to them.

The task of assembling the illustrations for this book was admirably discharged by Diane Casella Hines, Ellen Pronk, and Ellen Zeifer, all of whom, working in relays, also undertook to receive and manage the editing of waves of typescript, relayed from sea to shining sea. I owe them a measure of gratitude too vast to record properly here. The entire effort was sustained by the patience, wisdom, and generosity of spirit of my good friend Donald Holden, who also happens to be Editorial Director of Watson-Guptill Publications. I trust he will excuse me if I think of him here in more personal terms than is customary; his faith in this project transcended any official capacity as a publisher. Certainly no author could wish for, or need, better.

D.F.H.
San Francisco
April 1976

# LIST OF COLOR PLATES

# CONTENTS

# The
# Indigenous
# Tradition

THE golden age of American watercolor painting dawned in the late 19th century with Homer and Sargent and continued to advance well into the first decades of our own era, but there is abundant evidence that many distinguished artists who flourished earlier were thoroughly conversant with the medium.

In the early 19th century, American artists seemed to regard watercolor primarily as a mere sketching tool, or for use in creating preparatory drawings that only anticipated the "finished" work in oil or in a graphic medium such as engraving. In sharp contrast, English artists had fully embraced watercolor by the middle of the 18th century and had raised it to a position of serious endeavor equal to oil painting.

This attitude was slow to evolve among American artists until the genius of Winslow Homer revealed that watercolor had an extraordinary potential for serious expression. In the first decades of the 20th century, John Singer Sargent carried this potential seemingly to its farthest limits, manipulating watercolor with the same bravura that distinguished his work in oils. Watercolor was an inevitable medium for the American artist, who from the very beginning made landscape painting one of the dominant features of a national art tradition. The ability of the medium to combine rapidity of execution with its inherent luminosity gave the landscape painter an ideal means for recording the effects of nature directly.

Certain technical points about watercolor should be mentioned here, since the mastery of this difficult medium requires a thorough grounding by the practitioner, and the layman's appreciation of watercolor is enhanced by an understanding of its properties. And, while the evolution of watercolor technique was complete by the 19th century, it is useful to consider the history of its development, so far as concerns American art.

## Technique

Although watercolor is made of the simplest combination of materials, it is one of the most demanding mediums for the artist to manipulate successfully. Perhaps it is this seeming paradox that has intrigued the artist and the layman for so many centuries. Essentially, watercolor is nothing more than finely ground powdered pigment or dye suspended in an aqueous solution of gum arabic. Its normal condition is transparent; however, with the admixture of precipitated white chalk, it becomes gouache, an opaque medium. In both cases, ordinary water is the liquefying solvent.

Ideally watercolor is seen to best advantage in its transparent application, in which various colors are permitted to overlap, creating a system of glazes. Light is thereby reflected back from the underlying white paper through the transparent glazes, imparting the luminosity that is the special charm of watercolor. With the gouache technique, the artist may introduce a toned paper which, similar to the use of a toned canvas in oil painting, imparts an immediate unifying effect to the work when the ground is allowed to show through. Mixed techniques, in which combinations of transparent and opaque passages are used in a single work, are less satisfactory when the gouache passages are applied too vigorously and create an impasto that thwarts the purpose of working with a transparent medium. Gouache alone, however, can be effective in its own way—the matte finish of gouache can impart a handsome surface that modern artists, especially, have found enhances the aims of abstraction. Whether the paint is applied to wet or dry paper—toned or white—also affects the character of the work. Permanent artists' papers may be made of a variety of substances such as cotton, linen, mulberry bark, silk, or parchment.

The pigments used in watercolors are the same, generally, as those employed for oil paints. Earth pigments, vegetable dyes, and the various metallic oxides, abundant in nature, have long been in use. Before the development of modern chemistry in the early 19th century, certain colors could only be obtained from precious or semiprecious elements. The costly blue used in medieval illumination, for example, was produced from the semiprecious stone lapis lazuli. The introduction of coal-tar pigments in the 19th century not only expanded the range of available colors but also produced significantly brighter colors. Since the tendency of many pigments is to fade when exposed to light over a period of time, development of nonfading chemical pigments greatly enhanced the permanency of watercolors and all works of art.

## Watercolor in Europe

Watercolor has been generally in use by artists of the Western world for several centuries. As early as the 15th century, Albrecht Dürer (1471–1528) created remarkably naturalistic renderings in watercolor of animal and plant forms as well as landscape views of unusual inventiveness. Dürer's influence was felt in the Netherlands for a time and was partially responsible for the development there of what may be considered the first school of watercolor painting in Europe, led by Hans Bol (1534–93), Adriaen van Ostade (1610–85), and Albert Cuyp (1620–91). The tendency of the so-called Dutch "Little Masters," was to use watercolor as a decorative addition to what were essentially line drawings in ink or plumbago.

English artists began to take watercolor seriously for the first time in the early 17th century, following the arrival of Peter Paul Rubens (1577–1640) at the court of Charles I in 1629. But Rubens, who had been using watercolor to sketch landscape views for twenty years prior to his appearance in England, only gave further impetus to what had been gradually forming there. The English artist-explorer had already begun to point the way: in 1585 John White (active 1577–90) accompanied Sir Walter Raleigh to

Roanoke Colony in Virginia, where he made drawings in watercolor of the aboriginal inhabitants of the New World. White's work was published five years later by the German engraver Theodore de Bry as illustrations for *A Briefe and True Report of the New Found Land of Virginia*, and received wide attention.

Aside from the quasi-scientific purpose of this kind of drawing, other English artists began to use watercolor simply for recording portraits in miniature and even depicting landscapes. In the early 18th century, when the fashion of the grand tour of Italy began to be an important part of the cultural experience of the cultivated and affluent, English artists frequently accompanied gentlemen on these trips solely to provide a record of the places visited, much as one would take snapshots today. Their watercolor views of the crumbling remains of antiquity, brought back to England as souvenirs, helped to establish the esthetic of the "picturesque."

In the 18th century, the picturesque mode governed the style of domestic architecture and the elaborate landscape settings for the great English country houses, which were being created by that new professional, the landscape architect. Engraved views of the notable country houses of England, published by John Boydell (1719–1804) in London, not only spurred the public appetite for landscape art but also served to train many of his workers in the use of watercolor, since it was customary to tint the black and white engravings to make them more naturalistic and thus to increase their salability.

By the year of Boydell's death, watercolor painters had become so prominent in Britain that a group of sixteen founded a professional association known as the Society of Painters in Water Colours. Among them were the founders of the great tradition of 18th- and 19th-century watercolor in England: William Havell (1782–1851), known for his views of the Thames River; William F. Wells (1762–1836), the prime founder of the Society; and John Varley (1778–1842); considered the doyen of English watercolor painting. Organizations like the Society also came into being to solve the problem of showing watercolors in exhibitions, where they suffered alongside the generally stronger and larger works in oil. The various English watercolor societies boasted scores of artists whose fame increased the apparent sovereignty of that nation over the medium. The most distinguished of them were Paul Sandby (1730–1809), painter of romantic landscapes: William Gilpin (1762–1843), called the "Constable" of watercolor; John Sell Cotman (1782–1842), master of the flat wash; Thomas Girtin (1775–1802), painter of the Lake Country; David Cox (1783–1859), famous for his wild views of Wales; Peter de Wint (1784–1848), recorder of English farm life; Samuel Palmer (1805–81), whose early "visionary" style foreshadowed the Pre-Raphelites; Richard Parkes Bonington (1802–28), the consummate technician of the broken wash; Edward Lear (1812–88), famous for his Mediterranean views; and John F. Lewis (1805–76,

who specialized in figure paintings of the exotic Near East.

But Joseph Mallord William Turner (1775–1851), who made the revolutionary discovery that light is color and color is light, stands foremost as the great master of watercolor. Turner's mastery of the medium early in his career—learning, as he did, the use of translucent veils of color—enabled him subsequently to advance into the abstract grandeur of his oil paintings. Turner's great champion, John Ruskin, published his *Modern Painters* in an American edition in 1847, causing the full impact of Turner's achievements — as well as Ruskin's own philosophy of art—to be felt in the United States.

## American Watercolor in the 18th Century

In American art, there is only a very meager scattering of examples in watercolor in the 18th century. Of course, there exist works of a topographical nature, such as the *View of New Amsterdam*, 1660, by the obscure Dutch draughtsman Laurens Block, or the occasional city street scenes rendered by Cotton Milbourne (active 1794–1811), an immigrant English artist working in New York and Philadelphia.

Travel conditions in the American colonies may explain the seeming discrepancy between the habits of English artists and their American contemporaries in the 18th century. Highway connections between the principal English cities were well established in the 18th century, and travel was facilitated by regular services of Royal Mail coaches. Thus, English artists were free to travel and record what they saw — taking full advantage of the portability of watercolor equipment. However, no similar conditions existed in the American colonies. Even as late as 1750, travel by wagon between Philadelphia and New York required three days. In consequence, most extant views of the 18th century are of the eastern seaboard cities of Boston, New York, and Philadelphia.

## American Watercolor in the Early 19th Century

Through these eastern cities came immigrant artists from Europe, setting up their professions along the same lines they had followed abroad. One such family of artists — the English miniature painter and printmaker William R. Birch (1755–1834) and his son Thomas Birch (1779–1851) — settled in Philadelphia in 1794. There they reestablished the family business in printmaking. Birch's *Views of Philadelphia*, published in 1800, was the principal contribution to the fame of the son, who prepared the original watercolors, such as *Delaware River Front, Philadelphia* (see page 19). This work is the basis for one of the plates in the series — note the ruled-in squares for transfer. Birch's style derives from the traditional English approach to watercolor, with its careful drawing and even application of wash colors. John Lewis Krimmel (1789–1821), native of

Württemburg, Germany, also came to Philadelphia, and in 1810 he set up a studio for painting portraits. His fame, however, rests in the delightful and often gently satiric street scenes of that city. *Election Day at the State House* (see page 20), reveals his gift for social commentary, a quality that earned him the sobriquet, "the American Hogarth."

Benjamin Henry Latrobe (1764–1820) was an English engineer and architect who used watercolor in his renderings of proposed designs for clients. His most important client between 1803 and 1817 was the federal government. Hence, *U.S. Capitol, East Front, Perspective* (see page 21) is chiefly concerned with the formal relationships of the building itself and its relation to the site. But the crisp handling of the medium in Latrobe's hands is typical of the kind of pictorial elegance that continued to distinguish architectural renderings in watercolor throughout the 19th century.

The Irishman William Guy Wall (1792–after 1864) arrived in New York in 1818 and occupied himself during the next ten years with his watercolors of the Hudson River. Twenty of these works formed the basis for the celebrated suite of engravings, the *Hudson River Portfolio*, that enjoyed several editions between 1820 and 1828. His watercolor view of *New York Taken from Brooklyn Heights* (see page 21) incorporates Wall's typical delicacy of touch and is admirable for his technical control in a work of such relatively large dimensions.

Important also in the development of the popular taste for views of America is the graphic work of John Hill (1770–1850) and his son John William Hill (1812–79) who immigrated to the United States from England in 1819. The elder Hill is responsible for the engravings of Wall's watercolors for the *Hudson River Portfolio*, but his first major commission in America was a series of plates based on the paintings of Joshua Shaw, published as *Picturesque Views of American Scenery* in Philadelphia between 1820 and 1821. The son, John William Hill, is best known as a landscape and topographical painter. His street views such as *Broadway and Trinity Church* (see page 22) combine the qualities of the genre-oriented scenes of Krimmel and the architecturally dominated renderings of Latrobe.

## Urban Landscapes

The serenity that permeates the urban landscape pictures of the early 19th century is a reflection of the patronage of the middle class to whom the artist addressed his work. Certainly New York was no stranger to civil unrest or disaster, but the urban painters of the period remained aloof from any form of social commentary, preferring to work in the picturesque mode. Even the Neapolitan Nicolino V. Calyo (1799–1884), who journeyed from Baltimore especially to record the great fire of 1835—called the worst disaster of the century in New York—chose a distant view of the holocaust, reducing this catastrophe to a mere incidental in his otherwise placid prospect of the city and the bay (see page 23). Yet this work in gouache possesses a pictorial drama of another kind in its dramatic and finely balanced contrasts of masses, giving emphasis to the natural grandeur of a vast and open landscape that would be the dominant thrust of American art throughout the century.

This important aspect of the history was also a part of the work of George Harvey (c. 1800–78), whose experience as an immigrant from England to the frontier of Ohio, Michigan, and Canada decided his future career as an artist. About 1834 he began to paint what he called atmospheric views of American scenery in watercolor—he intended to publish some forty of these as engravings. Only four of the intended series were actually published — among them *Spring*, representing a scene in the Canadian wilderness (see page 24).

## Portraiture and Natural History Paintings

Besides the business of making topographical views, other avenues of endeavor attracted European artists to America. Portraiture became a thriving occupation in the early 19th century, occasioned by the rise of a growing middle class—before the era of the camera, the miniature portrait was a common possession. John Rubens Smith (1775–1849) brought with him from England an established career as a portrait painter, printmaker, and drawing teacher. During the 1830s he established a drawing academy in Philadelphia and was known for his high degree of technical accomplishment in watercolor, seen, for example, in the ingratiatingly informed portrait of an unknown Philadelphia physician (see page 25).

The most celebrated artist of all those who immigrated to America in this period did not embark upon a career in painting until several years after his arrival from France in 1806. When he did start painting, John James Audubon (1785–1851) developed an extraordinary body of work in watercolor as a consequence of his passionate interest in natural history. *Purple Grackle* (see Color Plate 1) is an original design for Robert Havell's brilliant engravings in Audubon's *Birds of America*, published in four volumes in London between 1827 and 1838. The enduring charm of Audubon's watercolors derives from his masterful compositions—the subjects transcend the limited interest of the natural historian and become genuinely esthetic experiences.

By the middle of the 19th century, chromolithography began to replace the various engraving techniques in producing popular prints. The Alsatian-born Christian Schussele-Sommerville (1824 or 1826–79) immigrated to Philadelphia from Paris in 1848, probably for political reasons during the revolutionary upheavals. Before turning to painting in oils in 1854 and beginning a long teaching career at the Pennsylvania Academy of Fine Arts — where he taught, among others, Thomas Eakins — Schussele worked at the chromolithographic trade. His marine life study (see page 26) is a work of exquisite realism, possibly prepared for full-color reproduction in a treatise on natural history.

## Folk, or Naive, Art

A strong tradition of indigenous art expression grew up with the colonies and the new nation. This so-called folk, or naive, art relied heavily on various watercolor methods, probably because the materials were less costly and more easily available than oil paints and canvas. Watercolor painting was regarded as part of the education of every cultivated young woman, who was schooled in what the early 19th century called female seminaries. These products of the folk art tradition abound even today in the form of still life, or theorem, paintings, so named because of their use of mechanical stencil patterns. Mourning pictures—watercolors depicting weeping figures at monuments inscribed with the name of a deceased loved one—were also favorite subjects for amateur painters of the early 19th century.

There is another level of artistic accomplishment generated from the folk tradition that is distinguished by a vigorous sense of design and color. Only a few such works are sufficient to indicate the range of accomplishment of the genius of the self-taught American amateur painter. Typically, the identities of many of these artists have become lost or only partially known from inscriptions—and such is the case with the painter of the portrait of *Elizabeth Fenimore Cooper* (see page 27). The subject's character is given an intense scrutiny, while the setting is delineated with an almost obsessive determination to master the difficulties of perspective. With much greater assurance, the unknown artist of *The Watercolor Class* (see Color Plate 2) describes another interior, providing a valuable record of the appearance' of a painting academy studio. This work and *Steamboat Chancellor Livingston* (see page 28) attest to the high degree of proficiency attained by what were essentially naive artists, influenced by the academic standards of the time.

Although his satirical wit was anything but naive, David Claypoole Johnston (1799–1865) worked so consistently in the flat linear manner of the folk tradition as to make his inclusion appropriate here (see page 29). As a book illustrator and printmaker, Johnston worked from his own watercolor drawings. He was known as the American Cruikshank, for his work always favored the same kind of barbed humor of the work of that famous Englishman whose painting style Johnston admired and imitated.

Joseph Davis (active 1832–37) is one of those rare identifiable itinerant folk artists thanks to the fact that he signed a few of his many pieces—he is known for over a hundred silhouette portraits made in rural Maine and New Hampshire. The itinerant painter of the early 19th century, traveling from village to town, often on foot, recorded the faces of a segment of American society not painted by the academic portrait painters of the great cities. His clients, who paid for his services in barter—

frequently exchanging food and lodging for his work—did not require a sophisticated performance. If the facial resemblance was correct—perhaps even naturalistic in execution — the accessory details needed only to be rendered schematically. The total effect, as in the double portrait of *James and Sarah Tuttle* (see page 30), presents a forceful pattern with a nearly abstract design.

The same taste lent itself to the decoration of the rural 19th-century parlor, which was often articulated by stencil patterns applied to plaster walls and painted wooden floors. *Fruit on Black Table* (see page 31), perhaps the work of an inspired student of some female seminary, would have perfectly complemented such an interior. Its unusual size and elegance indicate that the unknown folk artist may have had the work of some professional as his model. It is strongly suggestive of the still life paintings of Severin Roesen (active 1848 – 71), a recognized exhibitor in the New York galleries of the American Art–Union at the time this watercolor was created. In early colonial times, the self-taught artist frequently resorted to copying the engravings found in illustrated Bibles; in the 18th century he copied mezzotint engravings of European portraits; and in the 19th century he worked from engravings widely distributed by the various art union organizations.

## European Training

While most foreign-born artists arrived in America already skilled in their crafts, native Americans traveled to Europe seeking training and professionalism. When John Vanderlyn (1775 – 1852) was sent to Paris by his patron Aaron Burr, he found it more receptive to his particular genius than his native New York. At that time, 1796, no academy for the training of artists existed in New York, and would not until 1803, when John Trumbull established the American Academy of Fine Arts. Among Vanderlyn's most celebrated creations is *Ariadne*, which has been called the finest neoclassical nude by an American artist. Vanderlyn made many variations on this theme — one of the most charming is the watercolor destined for use as the working drawing for an engraver (see Color Plate 3). It is rendered with great delicacy, rather like a miniature, yet conveys the same assurance as the life-size version in oils painted at the same time which is now in the collection of the Pennsylvania Academy of the Fine Arts.

Running like a fever through 18th-century European culture, neoclassicism spawned not only the notion of the grand tour of Italy for aristocratic travelers but also the craving of dilettante artists to sketch the crumbling remains of the antique past in profusion. John Izard Middleton (1785–1849), born in Charleston, South Carolina but reared in England, passed most of his adult life in France and Italy. In 1812 he prepared the publication of his chief work, *Topographical and Picturesque Views of Ancient Latium,* a group of accomplished watercolors. His *View from the Summit of Monte Cavo*, a watercolor of ambitious size and thematic content, is at once an accurate, detailed topographical description and an intensely romantic work of art (see page 32). In quite a different vein, *Florence, A Sketch Made on the Ground* by Edward F. Peticolas (1793–c. 1853) is more like a leaf from a traveler's notebook—it is also somewhat modern in its simplification of forms (see page 33). Yet this view of the Duomo from the Boboli Gardens articulates the quality of Tuscan light and the glories of the past that would strongly attract generations of Americans in search of artistic roots.

In 1824 Robert Walter Weir (1803–89) went to Florence for a period of study that lasted three years —after which his work was almost exclusively concerned with historic events. In Europe he perfected a mastery of drawing that led to his appointment as instructor in that discipline at West Point, a post he held for some thirty years. *Sleeping Lute Player* (see page 34), painted during this tenure, is as much a recollection of his earlier study abroad as it is, perhaps, an obeisance to the kind of fashionable German genre painting widely acclaimed at the Düsseldorf Gallery in New York at that time.

Admiration for German art was the natural consequence for Emanuel Gottlieb Leutze (1816–68)— who was born in Germany and reared in America. In 1841 he returned to Germany and settled in Düsseldorf, then the center of the foremost school of historical narrative painting in Europe. Although he is best known today for his monumental painting *Washington Crossing the Delaware*, Leutze was an inveterate sketcher of nature. His *Cathedral Ruins* (see page 35), attests to his admiration for the work of Andreas Achenbach, one of the principal artists associated with Düsseldorf and its renowned Academy of Art.

Strong as its appeal was during the mid-19th century, the Düsseldorf style of dry, romantic realism did not exert a long-term influence on American art, in spite of Leutze's fame and that of his numerous compatriots who were its sometime disciples. The one American artist on whom the Düsseldorf style had profound influence was Richard Caton Woodville (1825–56). His brief career was completely devoted to the romantic narrative realism favored by Düsseldorf. But contrary to the tendency of that school of painting to immerse itself in the past, Woodville often chose to paint the genre of his own times. *Soldier's Experience* (see page 36), created in Baltimore the year before his departure for Europe, was converted in Düsseldorf into the oil painting *Old '76 and Young '48* on the occasion of the Mexican War.

The writings of the English critic John Ruskin and his advocacy of a national integrity in art appealed especially to American painters who, seeing worthy aspirations in their own traditions, were distrustful of overlong exposure to European influences. Ruskin's five-volume *Modern Painters,* the publication of which began in 1845, was initially a defense of the work of the English landscape painter, Joseph M. W. Turner; following its publication in the United States in 1847, the treatise became influential in the development of American art. The Irish-born James Hamilton (1819–1900) found an ideal model in Turner—clearly, his watercolors owe much to the study of Turner's brilliant use of the medium. During his lifetime, Hamilton was called the "American Turner," an apt though somewhat overstated description since Hamilton's marine watercolors (see page 37) depended on a more literal translation of nature. However, his most important commission—a set of glowing watercolors to illustrate Dr. Elisha Kane's two-volume *Arctic Explorations* published in 1855—alone would justify a comparison to Turner.

George Loring Brown (1814–89) was another American whose work earned him a sobriquet — "Claude" Brown, in reference to the 17th-century master Claude Lorraine, painter of expansive, luminous landscapes. Brown worked for twenty years in Florence and Rome, where he turned out a prodigious number of paintings in this vein. Though his oils tend to be ponderous in color and composition, many of Brown's watercolors, like the delightful *Near Rome* (see page 38), are convincing evocations of the mellow ambience of the Italian countryside.

The decades of the 1840s and 1850s in American art are marked by a surge of young artists going to Europe for long periods of study and travel. Most of them were not as closely identified with a particular place as Leutze had been with Düsseldorf or Brown with Rome. Jasper F. Cropsey (1823–1900) traveled extensively from the British Isles to the south of Italy, avoiding formal instruction and thus letting his own methods of painting govern the outcome of his work. In the summer of 1848, he shared a villa at Sorrento with the sculptor William Wetmore Story.

While Cropsey's style of painting seems to have been nearly fully formed by the time he arrived in Europe, the style of Worthington Whittredge (1820–1910) underwent profound changes. His five-year association with the international group of artists affiliated with the Düsseldorf Academy — and, more important, his friendship with the landscape painter Carl Frederick Lessing—gave his work a greater assurance than it had before his arrival in Europe. The taut, economical drawing of his *Landscape in the Harz Mountains* (see page 39) owes much to Lessing's guidance. Yet, in the end, Whittredge believed that no European academy could really improve upon native genius, and he ultimately championed the traditions of the Hudson River School of Thomas Cole and Asher B. Durand. The renewal of that tradition in the hands of the second generation of American painters provided the United States art with its chief attribute in the 19th century, the landscape painting.

## Landscape Painting

Charles Willson Peale (1741–1827) was one of the first Americans to fully appreciate and paint views of the Hudson River. Peale's sketchbook of 1801 (see Color Plate 4) contains a number of landscape studies in watercolor that reveal the delight he experienced: "The grand scenes . . . so enraptured me that I would, if I could, have made drawings with both hands at the same instant." Unlike most of the creations of his long career, Peale's Hudson River watercolors are spontaneous works. They show his awareness of well-ordered English landscape paintings in the medium, but their roughness accurately reflects the character of the American scene.

The Hudson Valley lay virtually unnoticed by artists for a quarter of a century before the appearance of Thomas Cole, the native genius of American landscape painting. Born the same year Peale made his historic Hudson River voyage, Cole emerged in 1825 from what was the frontier of Ohio and was immediately attracted to the scenery of the Hudson. The results of that first trip, displayed for sale in a New York shop window, so impressed his elders that John Trumbull, the eminent founder of the American Academy of Fine Arts, said to Cole upon their first meeting, "You surprise me, at your age, to paint like this. You have already done what I, with all my years and experience, am yet unable to do." For Cole had painted the reality of the American landscape, showing it as it was — untamed, wild and awesome, and wholly unlike the pacified views of nature favored by European artists.

In later years Cole's friend, the poet William Cullen Bryant, spoke of ". . . skies such as but Cole could ever paint, and through the transparent abysses of which it seemed that you might send an arrow out of sight." Bryant was speaking for a generation of painters who admired the quality of light that Cole had first seen and painted along the Hudson. This quality has come to be called luminism, and it is peculiar to American landscape painting in the mid-19th century. Cole was an avid sketcher who left many studies from nature in pen and ink. Regrettably, no finished composition in watercolor has yet been discovered.

At the same time Cole was painting, William Allen Wall (1801 – 85), was working in a somewhat old-fashioned way, taking the landscapes around the New England whaling town of New Bedford, Massachusetts for his subjects (see page 39). Wall's work is typical of an earlier manner of topographical rendering in watercolor — it is often based on highly romanticized recollections from earlier days rather than on actual observation.

Quite the opposite is the work of Asher B. Durand (1796 – 1886), whose achievements as a landscape painter rank him in importance second only to Cole. Indeed, Cole was the model upon whom Durand built his early career. Although Durand's watercolor A Woodland River (see page 40) does not rival the romantic intensity of Cole's best work, it accurately echoes the primary theme of the Hudson River School — the grandeur of untamed nature.

The disappearance of the American primeval forests was a threat anticipated by Cole. In his many essays for periodicals of the time, such as The American Monthly, Cole lamented the inevitability of their destruction. By mid-century, landscape views of the Hudson Valley assumed the fact of its nearly total domestication. William Ricarby Miller (1818 – 93) sketching his Catskill Clove (see page 41), worked in a controlled manner that belies his acquaintance with the work of some of his English contemporaries — particularly the Pre-Raphaelites — as much as it does his awareness of being surrounded by civilization.

By the mid-1800s, the pockets of remaining wilderness in the Hudson Valley, such as the Clove, became places of pilgrimage, visited by city-weary vacationers from New York, yearning to see untamed nature. Nostalgia was at the heart of much of the literature of the period as well. Washington Irving's Sketch Book of Geoffry Crayon contributed as much to the creation of legends of the Hudson Valley as it did to American letters. His country seat, Sunnyside (see page 42), painted the year after Irving's death by John Henry Hill (1839 – 1922) shows this gathering place of the New York literati as Irving had it remodeled in the manner of an "English cottage . . . strongly marked by symptoms of its Dutch origin . . ." by A. J. Davis, architect of many examples of revival houses, and friend of the writer. Hill's tightly rendered view is insistently topographical, and his watercolor technique returns, appropriately, to English prototypes.

Much of the same kind of domesticated scenery is found even in the works of the most devoted of the later Hudson River painters. Homer D. Martin (1836 – 97), whose paintings are among the final expressions of the true spirit of Cole, adopted the picturesque mode for his watercolor, Hudson River Scene (see page 43). And topographical views like Salem Common (see page 44) formed the basis for lithographic prints throughout the century that constituted the popular art of the times. In the hands of the ubiquitous Currier and Ives, the American landscape — rural as well as urban — became thoroughly synthesized into a kind of visual folklore.

American art in the period before 1860 was a remarkably integrated continuum, and those who studied abroad found themselves easily reunited with its native mainstream. From the art of the romantic realist Hudson River tradition, there emerged a new indigenous American style whose principal exponents — Martin J. Heade, Fitz Hugh Lane, and Frederic E. Church — had kept their eyes fixed steadfastly upon, as the poet Bryant had put it in a memorable phrase, "that wilder image" of American nature. Theirs was a shared interest in light, rather than any kind of school mannerism, that bound together their separate careers in the pursuit of what is known today as "luminism." Luminism sought to intensify reality through a heightened rendering of light and color in painting combined with a linear precision and extreme clarity of detail. During the decade of the 1860s, Martin Johnson Heade (1819 – 1904) directed most of his creative energies to the seemingly obsessive purpose of painting the effect of light at various times of the day on the Newburyport marshes of Massachusetts. One of his rare examples in watercolor of this subject, *Dawn* (see page 45), exemplifies the nearly scientific objectivity Heade directed toward the study of the effects of light—it serves to indicate the extent to which he and his fellow luminists unconsciously prefigured impressionism.

Ruskin's *Modern Artists* appeared in the United States in 1847. Its thesis espousing nationalism and the integrity of the artist tended to support rather than subvert the mainstream of American art as it had evolved from the loosely constructed aims of the Hudson River School. One of Ruskin's ardent American disciples was Charles Herbert Moore (1840 – 1930), whose position as an educator furthered the cause of Ruskin's teachings in America. The year he painted *Sawmill at West Boxford* (see page 45), Moore was appointed instructor of the principles of the fine arts at Harvard College, where he disseminated the esthetics of naturalism in art.

Clarity of execution in the rendering of nature was not only central to artists following the Ruskinian dogma, but was equally important to the realist-luminist direction of American art. William Trost Richards (1833 – 1905), who was briefly exposed to the academic routines at Düsseldorf in 1853, incorporated some of its "theatre of the picturesque" in the *Franconia Mountains* watercolor nearly twenty years later (see Color Plate 5). However, the dramatic simplifications of design in his well-known beach scenes find their ultimate source in a profound reverence for naturalism.

An important footnote to naturalism in the art of this period is the development of the camera — during the second half of the 19th century, artists worked contiguously with painting and photography. They tried to best the mechanical image with superior painted pictures of reality as well as to incorporate photography as a shortcut aid in the preparation of the painted picture. A hint of this is often present in Richards' marvelously able paintings of frozen wave action, such as in his *East Hampton Beach* (see page 46).

No mention of late 19th-century American marine painting would be complete without the mention of Alfred Thompson Bricher (1837–1908). Unfortunately, his marine watercolors seem inferior to his oils. Bricher excels in painting landscapes in gouache — the charm resulting from his judicious and sparkling distribution of color and the ingratiating mood is at the heart of works like *Summer Enchantment* and *At the Bridge* (see page 47 and Color Plate 6). Both were created at a time when Bricher was beginning to expand into figure painting; the former gouache became the study for a much larger oil painted in 1883.

## Genre Painting

Genre painting was the primary interest of Thomas Waterman Wood (1828 – 1903) for most of his career. His work bears a remarkable consistency throughout and indicates something about how insulated from change the American art world was before the 1880s and before the introduction of French Impressionism to the United States. Wood's mode of painting was symptomatic of the artistic intransigence to change and the deliberate attachment to the older romantic realist style that make his genre scenes seem old-fashioned even by the standards of his time (see page 48).

The same condition is evident in the later work of Jasper Cropsey, whose style had matured forty years before his *Early Snow, Mt. Washington* (see Color Plate 7), and in the work of William Stanley Haseltine (1835 – 1900), whose *Seal Harbor, Mt. Desert, Maine* (see page 49) maintains an almost Pre-Raphaelite purity of drawing. The paradigm of this tendency among some of the older academic realist painters was Edward Lamson Henry (1841 – 1919). His miniaturelike watercolors represent not only a style of painting frozen in its development years before but also a choice of subject matter that was insistently antiquarian. Few artists could match him technically, though, and Henry's small works in watercolor are among his finest achievements (see page 50).

## Paintings of the American West

The American West was an important area in the history of American art and of watercolor in particular. Much of the record of explorations and of the people of the lands west of the Mississippi was kept by artists whose only means of painting was watercolor. In 1803 President Thomas Jefferson authorized the exploration of this territory following the Louisiana Purchase, opening the initial period of westward expansion. George Catlin (1796–1870) was the first American artist of note to venture into the Great Plains, where he worked and traveled among various Indian tribes during the 1830s. While many of his landscapes are boldly executed, they tend to lack the precision and fidelity to life that were present in his incisive portraits of prominent Indian leaders (see page 51).

Alfred Jacob Miller (1810 – 74) spent only two years in the West recording the progress of the 1837-39 expedition led by the Scottish adventurer Sir William Drummond Stewart. Miller later translated his original sketches into finished watercolors and oils in his Baltimore studio—this is the case with *Lake Scene, Mountain of the Winds* (see page 52), the original version of which was painted in what is now western Wyoming. Miller's capacity to evoke the romance of the West expanded considerably through later reflection in the studio, and on this account his work lacks the realism of Catlin's life portraits.

One of the most popular painters of western life was Charles Deas (1818 – 67), whose works were constantly exhibited in the eastern art academies. Deas ventured to a frontier fort in Wisconsin in 1840 and soon moved to St. Louis, where he established a studio. In spite of his very brief exposure to formal instruction, Deas' highly romantic pictures of Mississippi River life seem to have been filtered through a literary sensibility (see page 53).

Standing in the greatest possible contrast to Deas, Seth Eastman (1808–75) worked in a style that was almost scientific in its detailed observation of Indian life. As a professional soldier, Eastman served in various capacities, first as a topographical engineer stationed on the western frontier and later as an instructor in drawing at West Point. His *Winnebago Wigwams* (see page 54) is probably an illustration for Henry Schoolcraft's monumental, six-volume *History and Statistical Information Respecting the . . . Indian Tribes of the United States.*

When the Civil War ended, the West entered a period of intense exploration, and settlement spread progressively toward the Pacific Ocean. A number of prominent, second-generation members of the Hudson River School were briefly attracted to these new vistas. By 1857, John F. Kensett, one of the dominant figures of the New York art establishment, had already ventured up the Missouri River. In 1886, Worthington Whittredge attached himself to an expedition of what is now Colorado and Mexico led by General John Pope.

Samuel Coleman (1832/33–1920), a distinguished member of the academic art establishment in New York who was once a student of Asher B. Durand, also traveled to the West. As first president of the American Society of Painters in Water Colors, Coleman was justly celebrated for his command of the medium. His command of the technique is well illustrated in the view of *The Green River, Wyoming* with its luminous atmospheric effects (see page 55).

Thomas Moran (1837–1926) made his first trip west in 1871 when he joined the Hayden surveying expedition. Subsequently, between 1872 and 1916, he made intermittent journeys into the western plains and mountains, which resulted in a seemingly endless succession of dramatic landscape paintings—Moran's name is indelibly fixed in history along with that of Albert Bierstadt as one of the two quintessential painters of the American West. Both of these artists brought a stylistic elegance to their paintings, which were intended as salon pictures. Moran's admiration for Turner, in particular, comes through forcefully in a series of glowing watercolors depicting Yellowstone National Park (see page 89 and Color Plate 20).

Moran, like so many artists of his time, often resorted to photographs but concealed the fact in his painterly style. Henry Farny (1847–1916), on the other hand, makes a more overt use of photography in his tightly drawn and naturalistic painting. With his experience as an illustrator for *Harper's Weekly* and *Century Magazine,* Farny was keen at observing detail. His paintings and watercolors of the lives of the Plains Indian are among the most accurately observed records existing (see page 56).

**Delaware River Front, Philadelphia** *by Thomas Birch. 10⅛" x 13⅞"/25.72 x 35.24 cm. Courtesy Museum of Fine Arts, Boston, Massachusetts, M. and M. Karolik Collection.*

**Election Day at the State House** *by John Lewis Krimmel, 1816. 8½″ x 13″/21.59 x 33.02 cm. Courtesy the Historical Society of Pennsylvania, Philadelphia, Pennsylvania.*

**U.S. Capitol, East Front, Perspective** *by Benjamin Henry Latrobe, 1810. Pencil, pen and ink, and watercolor, 17" x 25-7/16"/43.18 x 64.61 cm. Maryland Historical Society, Baltimore, Maryland, The Papers of Benjamin Henry Latrobe.*

**New York Taken from Brooklyn Heights** *by William Guy Wall, c. 1820–1825. 21-5/16" x 32¾"/54.13 x 83.18 cm. Metropolitan Museum of Art, New York, Bequest of Edward W. C. Arnold, 1954.*

**Broadway and Trinity Church** *by John W. Hill, 1830. 9-10/16" x 13-10/16"/ 24.45 x 34.61 cm. New York Public Library, Prints Division, The I.N. Phelps Stokes Collection, Astor, Lenox, and Tilden Foundations.*

**View of the City of New York, Governor's Island, Taken from Brooklyn Heights on the Morning after the Conflagration** *by Nicolino Calyo, c. 1835. Gouache, 19¾" x 25-11/16"/50.16 x 65.25 cm. Metropolitan Museum of Art, New York, Bequest of Edward W. C. Arnold Collection of New York Prints, Maps, and Pictures, 1954.*

**Spring—Burning Up Fallen Trees—A Girdled Clearing—Canada** *by George Harvey, c. 1841. 13⅞″ x 10¼″/35.24 x 26.04 cm. The Brooklyn Museum, Brooklyn, New York, Dick S. Ramsay Fund.*

**Philadelphia Physician** *by John Rubens Smith, 1838. 17" x 13-1/16"/43.18 x 33.18 cm.*
*Courtesy Museum of Fine Arts, Boston, Massachusetts, M. and M. Karolik Collection.*

**Untitled watercolor** *by Schussele-Sommerville. Collection of Mr. and Mrs. Erving Wolf.*

**Portrait of Elizabeth Fenimore Cooper** *by "Mr. Freeman," c. 1816. 17½" x 21½"/44.45 x 54.61 cm. Courtesy New York State Historical Association, Cooperstown, New York.*

**Steamboat Chancellor Livingston,** *Anonymous, 1822. 19⅞″ x 30⅞″/50.48 x 78.42 cm. Collection Albany Institute of History and Art, Albany, New York.*

**Militia Muster** *by David Claypoole Johnston, c. 1828. 10¾" x 15"/27.3 x 38.1 cm.*
*Courtesy American Antiquarian Society, Worcester, Massachusetts.*

**James and Sarah Tuttle** *by Joseph H. Davis, 1836. 9½" x 14½"/24.13 x 36.83 cm.*
*Courtesy the New-York Historical Society, New York.*

**Fruit on Black Table.** *Unknown American artist. 1854. 29″ x 40⅞″/73.7 x 103.8 cm.*
*Collection of Whitney Museum of American Art, New York, Gift of Edgar William*
*and Bernice Chrysler Garbisch.*

**View from the Summit of Monte Cavo** *by John Izard Middleton, 26" x 48"/66 x 121.92 cm. Collection of Susan Middleton Rutledge Moore.*

**Florence, A Sketch Made On the Ground** *by Edward F. Peticolas, c. 1853. 10¾" x 14⅞"/27.3 x 37.78 cm. The Valentine Museum, Richmond, Virginia.*

**Sleeping Lute Player** *by Robert Walter Weir, c. 1850. 13⅝" x 9¾"/34.61 x 24.76 cm. Courtesy Museum of Fine Arts, Boston, Massachusetts, M. and M. Karolik Collection.*

**Cathedral Ruins** *by Emanuel Leutze, c. 1845. Wash, 10½" x 14½"/26.67 x 36.83 cm.*
*In the Collection of the Corcoran Gallery of Art, Washington, D.C.*

**Soldier's Experience** *by Richard Caton Woodville, May 1844. 11" x 10"/27.94 x 25.4 cm. Walters Art Gallery, Baltimore, Maryland.*

**Marine** *by James Hamilton, c. 1850. 11" x 17"/27.94 x 43.18 cm. The Brooklyn Museum, Brooklyn, New York, Gift in Memory of Donald W. Stark.*

**Near Rome** *by George Loring Brown, 1857. 8-5/16" x 11⅞"/21.11 x 30.16 cm. The Brooklyn Museum, Brooklyn, New York, Dick S. Ramsay Fund.*

**Landscape in the Harz Mountains** *by Worthington Whittredge, 1852. Watercolor and pencil, 13-9/16 /34.45 x 50.01 cm. Collection of Mr. and Mrs. E. P. Richardson, Philadelphia, Pennsylvania.*

**View in New Bedford, Massachusetts** *by William Allen Wall. 11¼" x 18⅛"/28.58 x 46.04 cm. Courtesy Museum of Fine Arts, Boston, Massachusetts, M. and M. Karolik Collection.*

**A Woodland River** *by Asher B. Durand. 19⅜" x 25"/49.01 x 63.5 cm. Courtesy Museum of Fine Arts, Boston, Massachusetts, M. and M. Karolik Collection.*

**Catskill Clove** *by William Ricarby Miller, 1856, 19⅞″ x 14¾″/50.48 x 37.46 cm.*
*Metropolitan Museum of Art, New York, Gift of Mrs. A. M. Miller, 1893.*

**"Sunnyside" in 1860, Tarrytown, New York** *by John Henry Hill, 1860. 10" x 13-9/16"/25.4 x 34.45 cm. Courtesy Museum of Fine Arts, Boston, Massachusetts. M. and M. Karolik Collection.*

**Hudson River Scene** *by Homer D. Martin, before 1882. 9½" x 16½"/24.13 x 41.91 cm. New York State Historical Association, Cooperstown, New York.*

**Salem Common,** *Anonymous, 1863. 11½" x 16½"/29.01 x 41.91 cm. Courtesy Museum of Fine Arts, Boston, Massachusetts, M. and M. Karolik Collection.*

**Dawn** *by Martin Johnson Heade, c. 1865–1870. 32¾" x 21½"/83.18 x 54.61 cm. Private Collection.*

**Sawmill at West Boxford** *by Charles Herbert Moore, c. 1874. 11⅞" x 18"/30.16 x 45.72 cm. The Art Museum, Princeton University, Princeton, New Jersey.*

**East Hampton Beach** *by William Trost Richards. 1871 – 1874. 18" x 32"/45.72 x 81.28 cm. Permanent Collection of The High Museum of Art, Atlanta, Georgia, Gift of Mr. and Mrs. Emory L. Cocke, 1970.*

**Summer Enchantment** *by Alfred T. Bricher, 1878. Gouache, 14½" x 20⅞"/36.83 x 53.02 cm. Private Collection, New York.*

**The Wanderer** *by Thomas Waterman Wood, 1874. 14" x 10"/35.56 x 25.4 cm.*
*Courtesy Museum of Fine Arts, Boston, Massachusetts, M. and M. Karolik Collection.*

**Seal Harbor, Mt. Desert, Maine** *by William Stanley Haseltine. 14¼" x 21½"/36.2 x 54.61 cm. The University of Georgia, Georgia Museum of Art, Athens, Georgia, Gift of Helen Haseltine Plowden, 1961. Courtesy of the National Academy of Design.*

**Entering the Lock** *by Edward Lamson Henry, 1899. 11" x 19¾"/27.94 x 50.16 cm.*
*Collection Albany Institute of History and Art.*

**The Smoke Shield** *by George Catlin. 10⅛" x 8½"/25.72 x 21.59 cm. Anonymous loan.*

**Lake Scene, Mountain of the Winds** *by Alfred Jacob Miller, 1837. 9-3/16" x 13-9/16"/23.34 x 34.45 cm. The Walters Art Gallery, Baltimore, Maryland.*

**The Trapper and His Family** *by Charles C. Deas. 13⅜" x 19½"/33.97 x 49.53 cm.*
*Courtesy Museum of Fine Arts, Boston, Massachusetts, M. and M. Karolik Collection.*

**Winnebago Wigwams** *by Seth Eastman, 1850. 7" x 10"/17.78 x 25.4 cm. Peabody Museum, Harvard University, Cambridge, Massachusetts.*

**The Green River, Wyoming** *by Samuel Coleman, 1871. Watercolor and pencil,
16" x 21¾"/40.64 x 55.24 cm. Courtesy Museum of Fine Arts, Boston, Massachusetts,
M. and M. Karolik Collection.*

**In Pastures New** *by Henry Farny, 1895. Gouache, 14½″ x 27½″/36.83 x 69.85 cm. Collection of Frank B. Cross III.*

**Indian Encampment** *by Henry Farny. 4½″ x 8″/11.43 x 20.32 cm. Anonymous loan.*

# The
# Influence
# of Europe

THE year 1850 may be considered the beginning of a new epoch in American art, with respect to the development of watercolor painting. On Christmas Day of that year, a group of thirty artists gathered in the studio of John Falconer on Hudson Street in New York and drafted both a constitution and bylaws, establishing "The Society for the Promotion of Painting in Water Color." In addition to securing an exhibition space in the Library Society building in lower Manhattan, the Society also founded a small school for the instruction of watercolor painting. Periodic exhibitions of the members' paintings also included works by noted English artists of the day, borrowed from embryonic private collections in the city. The Society's activities also included organized sketching excursions along the Hudson River. Its major public exposure came in 1853 when the Society presented works by its members in the "Industry of All Nations" section of the Crystal Palace Exposition in New York.

The Society did not prosper, however, and, by the time of its annual meeting in 1854 membership had fallen to twenty-one. The group gave up its quarters in the Library Society building and returned to Falconer's studio, where it broke up amid dissention. No further attempt to formally organize the growing numbers of watercolor painters in New York was made for another decade. During that decade, though, Henry Warren's *Painting in Water Color* was published in New York in 1856 — the book was a considerable improvement over the only other manual of instruction existing at the time, *Elements of Graphic Art,* by Archibald Robertson, published in 1802 and by the 1850s long out of print.

## History of the American Watercolor Society

In the fall of 1866 the National Academy of Design was host to an exhibition of watercolor painting in its elaborate neo-Venetian Gothic building on 23rd Street in New York, sponsored by an independent group called The Artists Fund Society. Within a few months of this event, forty-two prominent artists living in and near New York founded "The American Society of Painters in Water Colors." About one-third of these artists were already members of the National Academy of Design; others had been members of the defunct watercolor society that ceased to exist around 1854.

This resurgence of interest in watercolor may be traced to the important part artist-reporters played in the Civil War. Alfred R. Waud and Winslow Homer were widely known for their on-the-scene drawings of wartime action; many of their wash watercolors were published as cover illustrations for *Harper's Weekly.* They and others of a more political bent, like Thomas Nast, helped shape the public attitude of the North toward the war, while—not incidentally — contributing toward the expanding development of graphic art in America.

Immediately after it was founded, The American Society of Painters in Water Colors published a pamphlet entitled "Water Color Painting: Some Facts and Authorities in Relation to Its Durability." The purpose of this pamphlet was to inform the general public about the special properties of watercolor—it was probably useful in generating sales at the first exhibition of the Society at the National Academy of Design during the winter of 1867–68.

Many English authorities and artists were cited in the pamphlet—George Barret, a founder of the English Water Colour Society, was among them. Barret discussed the question of the permanency of watercolor, pointing out that methods inherited from the 18th century — including the preparation of a picture in gray undertones using fugitive pigments like India ink or indigo — were largely responsible for criticism concerning the durability of the medium. He advised against such preparatory methods and advocated instead a direct approach, using a "liberal supply" of colors. Thus the Society urged the spontaneous execution of watercolors as opposed to elaborate drawing. This interpretation gradually led to the general recognition of watercolor as an independent painting medium different from, but equal to, the oil technique — and watercolor began to be regarded as suitable for serious artistic expression.

Beginning in 1867 with its first president, Samuel Coleman, the society was closely associated with the National Academy of Design. Coleman's successors, William Hart (1823–94), elected in 1870, and James D. Smillie (1833–1909), elected in 1873, were both landscape painters and carried on the traditional association between the two groups. In 1878, two major changes occurred. The Society held its annual exhibition at the Brooklyn Art Association; this event marked the first time the group exhibited separately from the National Academy. The exhibition drew 490 entries, making it one of the most ambitious shows to that date. It attracted the participation of such distinguished artists as James A. McNeill Whistler, Thomas Eakins, and Edwin A. Abbey.

The year 1878 also marked the election of Thomas W. Wood as president of the Society, which changed its name at this point to the less pretentious "American Water Color Society." Wood, the painter of homely genre subjects, was succeeded in the presidency in 1887 by the most popular genre painter of that generation, John G. Brown (1831–1913), who served in office for almost twenty years. The annual exhibition of 1888 established the precedent of competition for prizes, placing the American Water Color Society on a professional level with the National Academy of Design and ensuring its place as a major influence in the New York art world.

Like the National Academy, the Society tended to be a preserve for men, severely limiting the numbers of women admitted to membership. Largely as a result of this, the New York Watercolor Club came into existence in 1889 with Childe Hassam as its first president. Significantly, the first meeting of the new club was held in the studio of a woman artist, Julia

Baker. Hassam, who had recently returned from study in France, undoubtedly brought back with him an appreciation of the important role played by women in French culture, among them the American expatriate painter Mary Cassatt (1845–1926). The first exhibition of the Club was held in the American Art Galleries, a commercial establishment on Madison Square. Only four years earlier, the French art impresario Paul Durand-Ruel had successfully presented the first major exhibition of French impressionism to the American public in that same gallery.

In 1895 Hassam joined forces with another group of artists who had embraced Impressionism and exhibited in New York, calling themselves "Ten American Painters." "The Ten," as they came to be known, preferred the pastel medium when not working in oils. Except for Hassam, they did not contribute importantly to the history of American watercolor painting. Others, however, working independently of The Ten in the impressionist mode attained great distinction as masters of watercolor—particularly James A. McNeill Whistler, John La Farge, and John Singer Sargent.

By the turn of the century, the American Water Color Society was holding its annual exhibitions at the Waldorf-Astoria Hotel, having abandoned the Brooklyn Art Association for a more central location in keeping with its growing national prestige. Such was the demand upon its facilities as a national showcase for contemporary watercolor painting that in 1905 the Society established a system of rotary exhibitions. This meant that, henceforth, the annual exhibition would not be limited geographically to New York—after an initial showing in that city, it would travel to St. Louis, Cincinnati, Indianapolis, Detroit, and Buffalo.

The responsibility for arranging this ambitious program was assigned to the staff at the St. Louis Museum of Fine Arts, which attempted to deal with the growing complexity of the Society's business. By 1913 the scope of activity had so enlarged that the task of organizing traveling exhibition programs was taken over by the Fine Arts Federation of Washington, D.C. The next year the Society began to absorb the New York Watercolor Club into its exhibition program, a policy that led inexorably to a merger of the two organizations in 1941 under the single name "American Watercolor Society."

## Romantic Landscapes

The American artist's increasing involvement in the latter half of the 19th century with Continental painting, rather than with purely English styles, marks a gradual change in American art. In general, the linear luminist manner of the native tradition evolved into a more sensuous approach to painting. One of the first Americans to respond to this change was George Inness (1825–94), whose innate emotionalism led him to attempt greater expressiveness and to modify the Cole-Durand pictorial vocabulary.

Following his third trip to Europe in 1859, Inness began to translate his devotion to the romantic landscapes of the Barbizon painters into a new vision of the American landscape. He settled in rural Medfield, Massachusetts, evolving a manner of painting that is richly atmospheric and determinedly painterly. His watercolors do not convey his concern for the tactile values of oil impasto, but *Trout Stream,* from the Medford period, conveys Inness' ability to achieve the romantic mood of nature (see page 68).

## Winslow Homer

Winslow Homer (1836–1910) began his career much the same way as Inness. After beginning in Boston as a self-taught illustrator, Homer was profoundly affected by a ten-month trip to France in 1867. He incorporated a certain plein air impressionist vision in the first paintings he made after returning to the United States, but that seems to have been but a momentary flirtation with mannerisms acquired perhaps from an observation of the work of Edouard Manet and Frédéric Bazille. Thereafter, he quickly amalgamated this experience with his own romantic realist vision, producing a more painterly style than he had employed before.

Homer's first serious work in watercolor came in the early 1870s, and much of his subject matter of that period is a restatement of themes he used earlier in his illustrations for *Harper's Weekly.* One of these, *Seven Boys in a Dory* (see page 69), betrays a certain hesitancy with the watercolor medium; its rather hard application of washes seems granular in texture, as if following the preliminary pencil drawing. By the summer of 1875, Homer rapidly modified the technique used in this work, made in Gloucester, Massachusetts while on assignment for *Harper's Weekly.* At that time, Homer created a prodigious amount of work based on rural life in upstate New York. One of this series, *The Trysting Place* (see page 70), reveals his growing command of the watercolor medium. The separate acts of drawing and painting began to fuse into a single act, manifesting itself in pictures in a more painterly character—his former linear treatment of forms was replaced by a greater attention to mass and atmosphere.

By the time Homer returned to Europe to live in seclusion at Tynemouth, England in the early 1880s, he had nearly mastered the fluid, yet solid manner that distinguishes his best watercolors. Yet the literary content of his subject matter continued to dominate his work; the critic Henry James, reviewing Homer's work during the 70s, found this a "damnably ugly" problem.

The two years Homer worked in Tynemouth wrought subtle and profound changes in his art. He had time to consider man's fate at the mercy of an impersonal and hostile nature; for the first time, the theme of the tragic confrontation between man and the sea emerged to dominate his work. *Fisher Girl* (see page 71) is one of many drawings and water-colors that share the elegiac quality of Homer's Tynemouth experience.

When he returned to the United States, Homer gravitated to the isolation of a small community on the Maine coast, Prout's Neck. There he embarked upon a lifelong search for an accommodation of the conflict he saw between the elemental forces of nature and the human condition. He portrayed this conflict in the watercolor *The Ship's Boat* (see page 71), using the same stark terms with which he invested his greatest oil paintings.

Winslow Homer ranks among the greatest painters America has produced, a status accorded him not by posterity alone but also by his contemporaries. An artist of extraordinary profundity, he has the ability to affect the humblest admirer of his art as well as the most worldly connoisseur. His best watercolors are at once consummate technical performances of a master of the medium and deeply moving statements about his emotional responses to nature. Homer conveyed those responses with such conviction, boldness, and vigor that he compels the viewer to accept his vision of the world as reality. The freshness and palpable realism of *Leaping Trout* (see page 72) and *The Mink Pond* (see Color Plate 8) seem to deny all temporal considerations—they are timeless.

Homer's passion for outdoor life was a complex experience—since artist and sportsman are joined in him, his paintings of hunting and fishing scenes ring true to life. The Adirondack Mountains of New York were one of Homer's favorite vacation retreats during the 1890s. From this rugged region inhabited by backwoodsmen, fishing guides, and hunters, Homer derived some of his most memorable themes — powerful images full of a notable starkness and simplicity of design, yet redolent of the sensuousness of pine and hemlock woods (see pages 73 and 74). There is an exactness of feeling in *Hunter in the Adirondacks* (see Color Plate 9) that is achieved through an unerring sense for the quality of light and Homer's intuitive perception of the character of abstract forms.

Toward the end of his life, Homer sought the warmth of the Caribbean and Bermuda during the winter months. The islands offered relaxation from the arduous months in his Prout's Neck studio where, as America's most celebrated painter, he fended off unwanted visitors while creating a succession of masterpieces of painting. His watercolors of the tropics speak of the delight he found in the azure skies, the shimmering transparent shallows of the islands, and the warm overhead sun (see page 75). When he painted scenes of native life, his objectivity was constant. *Sponge Fishing, Bahamas* (see Color Plate 10) is typical of these tropical genre subjects—Homer does not idealize, nor does he indulge in the picturesque. Although his methods were not so simple as he would have had the world believe ("When I have selected [the subject] carefully, I paint it exactly as it appears . . ."), they resulted in paintings with an often deceptive immediacy. This was the consequence of the innate directness of his vision coupled with a superlative technical command of the medium.

After the turn of the century, Homer preferred Florida for his winter respite from labor at Prout's Neck. He was fond of the bass fishing on the Homosassa River, and his many watercolors of that swampland convey a feeling of the oppressive humidity and the mystery of its mangrove jungles (see Color Plate 11). These late examples, often painted during bouts of failing health, do not have the coloristic brilliance of his earlier works and strike a somewhat somber note in a career crowded with more robust creations. Yet, nearing the end of his productive years, Homer summoned forth one last effort in a burst of creative energy. *Diamond Shoal*, his last watercolor (see Color Plate 12), is a summation of the artist's best qualities: boldly conceived, directly observed, and apparently spontaneous, the work is a challenge to the technical abilities of future watercolor painters, all of whom owe him an acknowledgment for his influence on their development. Homer's own estimate of his attainments was characteristically shrewd. According to his first biographer, William H. Downes, pressed for an answer to the question of what he considered his greatest work, Homer responded, "You will see, in the future I will live by my watercolors."

## Thomas Eakins and his Followers

Thomas Eakins (1844–1916) began painting in watercolor about the same time as Homer, but he only worked in the medium for a little more than ten years of his career. Thus Eakins' watercolors are remarkably consistent in style and quality; moreover, they constitute an important part of his systematic investigations into the craft of painting. As a student at the Pennsylvania Academy of the Fine Arts in Philadelphia in the early 1860s, Eakins admired the work of the French academic painter, Jean-Louis Gérôme, a master of exact drawing. In 1866 Eakins went to Paris, where he became one of Gérôme's most dedicated pupils. To this experience, he added an intense study of the great Spanish realists of the 17th century, particularly Velásquez and Ribera. Eakins' many letters from Europe constantly refer to "solid painting"; he was studying the masters not in order to borrow styles of painting, but to gain insight into the achievement of realism in painting. His intellect was inquiring and analytical; his dedication to obtaining truth to life in his paintings approached a kind of passion.

Eakins' watercolors are unique in the history of American art. Of the fewer than twenty known examples, nearly half are the result of meticulous studies in oil, a reversal of the customary practice. Eakins regarded watercolor as the ultimate medium for conveying the illusion of natural light. For *John Biglen in a Single Scull* (see page 76) Eakins made both preparatory oil studies and a grisaille drawing, in which the artist carefully plotted the perspective of the scene. In his classes on perspective at the Pennsylvania Academy, Eakins lectured his students on the absolute necessity for mastering this science, which he regarded as second only to the study of anatomy as the basis for sound painting.

Nowhere in his work does Eakins achieve such a convincing illusion of broad daylight as in *Whistling for Plover* (see Color Plate 13), the ultimate statement in his study of naturalistic effects of light and atmosphere. By the middle of the 1870s, though, Eakins began to turn away from these sporting scenes. As his work became more introspective, his interest shifted to closed space — he enveloped portraits and figure studies in the dim light of his studio, and his work took on an Old Master chiaroscuro effect. Perhaps this was the result of the failure of his greatest painting — *The Gross Clinic* of 1875 — to gain critical favor. Eakins subsequently retreated to an increasingly private existence.

*Seventy Years Ago* (see page 77) is a calculated nostalgia piece, an attempt to recreate the spirit of the Federal era that recalls pictures like Gilbert Stuart's *Portrait of Mrs. Seymour Fort.* It is part of a series of oils and watercolors painted around the time of the Centennial Exposition in Philadelphia, which engendered a general popularity for and revival of Colonial styles. In spite of its modest size and meticulous drawing — qualities shared by almost all of Eakins' watercolors — this genre study communicates the same monumentality of form and humanist perception of character found in his more ambitious oil portraits. Above all, Eakins' watercolors demonstrate his ability to transcend the limitations of academic discipline and to create works of great poetic beauty.

Although Eakins was one of the greatest teachers of his time and had been prominent first at the Pennsylvania Academy and later at the Art Students League of Philadelphia, he did not attract many true disciples. William J. McCloskey (ca. 1860 – early 1900s), an obscure but able painter, came briefly under Eakins' influence. McCloskey's known works are still life paintings, a field that apparently held no interest for Eakins. *Still Life with Mandarin Oranges* (see page 78) exists also in an oil version of nearly identical size, a fact that suggests Eakins' use of preparatory oil studies. Moreover, the crisply rendered forms and the manner in which the background is painted in point conclusively to Eakins' influence.

Still life was never a particularly popular subject for watercolor painters; the absence of distance mitigates the effect of the transparent glazes, which create atmospheric effects. Solidity of form, the principal aim of still life, is best obtained in the oil medium. However, the trompe l'oeil still lifes of Claude Raguet Hirst (1855 – 1942) — she is known solely for her sensitively observed and charmingly intimate watercolors — show that success in this combination of subject and medium is possible (see Color Plate, 14). Hirst was the only important member of the 19th-century American still life tradition that included William M. Harnett and John F. Peto, who painted in watercolor. All of these artists are related to the Philadelphia school of still life painting that originated early in the 19th century with the works of James and Raphaelle Peale.

## Influence of European and Oriental Art

By the third quarter of the century, a steady stream of American artists went abroad to study in Munich and Paris. For William Keith (1838/39 – 1911), Düsseldorf was still attractive since landscape painting continued to flourish there in 1870, in spite of the decline of its once-popular Academy. Before and after Düsseldorf, Keith's interests took him to the American West. The examples of Leutze and Albert Bierstadt — both artists intimately connected with Düsseldorf who became celebrated as painters of the western landscape — probably guided Keith's choice of schooling. *The Lone Pine,* probably a California scene, shows strong influences of the Düsseldorf penchant for theatrical effects and crisp linear style of drawing (see page 79).

James Wells Champney (1843 – 1903) made periodic visits to Europe throughout his career — this habit became especially frequent after 1880, when he maintained a studio in Paris. Primarily an illustrator, Champney was an avid sketcher in watercolors. His *Artist Sketching in a Park* (see page 78), with its muted yet resonant washes, reveals his strong admiration for French Impressionism.

Trained in Munich, William M. Chase (1849 – 1916) combined the slashing brushwork style of that realist school with an impressionist palette after 1880, creating some of the best plein air paintings produced in America. As a teacher at the Art Students League in New York and later at his own painting school, Chase imparted his special brio style to a large following of students. In portrait painting, Chase's only rival was John Singer Sargent. Chase's work in watercolor, though not so well known as his oils, bears the same stamp of his forceful personality (see page 80).

By the turn of the century, a kind of composite of romantic realism and impressionism became thoroughly accepted as the vernacular expression of American art. Thomas Anshutz (1851 – 1912), who had been the spiritual heir of Eakins' academic realism as well as his successor at the Pennsylvania Academy, turned away from the master's sober objectivity to the charms of impressionism. Anshutz reveals himself as a true poet of light and atmosphere, especially in the watercolors done while on holiday in New Jersey, such as *Two Boys by a Boat* (see page 81).

A strong figurative strain remained at the heart of American painting, however — few artists who regarded themselves nominally as impressionists ever went as far as their French contemporaries in dissolving subject matter in light and color. The antithesis of the impressionist fever was the work of Edwin A. Abbey (1852 – 1911), a prodigious illustrator and mural painter. His exquisite command of drawing was reinforced in his paintings by a rich, decorative color sense, a reflection of his admiration for the English Pre-Raphaelite painters. Especially in his watercolors, where the size of the work equals that of his celebrated pen and ink drawings, Abbey achieved a subtle fusion of line and color (see Color Plate 15).

Less consistent in his many careers as illustrator, painter of easel pictures, and muralist, Robert Blum (1857 – 1903) alternated between romantic realism and neoclassicism. His early training in Paris under Gérôme and Fortuny indoctrinated him with the tendency toward sentimental narrative of the Academie des Beaux-Arts, where he went for study in 1880. Blum's subsequent work as an illustrator for *Scribner's Magazine* took him to Japan in 1890, where he applied a thoroughly Beaux-Arts style of genre painting to recording scenes of street life (see page 81). Blum's art was untouched by *Japonisme*, though, a peculiarly Western assimilation of Oriental modes of composition and color that took hold of French art in the late 19th century and found its ultimate expression in art nouveau.

In the historic conversion of the rediscovered principles of Oriental art—such as occult balance, or asymmetry, and flat, two-dimensional design — to modern usage, James A. McNeill Whistler (1834 – 1903) played a major part. American by birth, he became a lifelong expatriate at twenty, never to return to the United States. From his studios in Paris and London, he had a profound impact on the development of modern art. Whistler's adaptation of the elements of Japanese design to his painting was creative rather than imitative; he blended its then-novel flat patterning with a highly personal, impressionist interpretation of nature.

While his portraits (see page 82) tell of an additional ingredient — a deep admiration for the portraits of Velásquez — Whistler's landscape subjects are as much a celebration of nature's varying moods as are the quite different works of the French Impressionists. Whistler searched in directions not taken by French art of the period; his paintings, conceived as unified tonal statements, contain none of the brilliant color of plein air impressionism. As E. P. Richardson has pointed out, Whistler was working separately in Europe toward the same ends and at the same time as the American "Tonalist" painters of the poetry of mood; but Whistler was unaware of that late development of American luminist art flourishing at the turn of the century.

By the late 1860s, Whistler was already evolving a highly individual style of painting, one that tended to subordinate subject matter to mood more and more. By 1872 he had established the dual objective of his paintings by giving a commissioned portrait the subtitle, "Symphony in Flesh Color and Pink." Thereafter, his paintings focused on the poetry of mood, and Whistler gradually eliminated specific details in favor of a purely emotional response to nature in general. His celebrated nighttime painting of London's Cremorne Gardens during a fireworks display, *Nocturne in Black and Gold — The Falling Rocket* (c. 1874), became one of the great causes célèbres of modern art when the aging critic John Ruskin attacked the work and its creator, implying fraudulent intent. The resulting libel action by Whistler against Ruskin, though won by the artist, was only a symbolic victory. But the event did establish the principle of the artist's inherent right to self-expression.

Whistler went on to create paintings and pastels of increasing simplification of form and content. His watercolors were a product of his maturity, fine intelligence, and subtle perception. *The Nocturne: Grand Canal, Amsterdam* (see Color Plate 16) utilizes the liquid properties of the medium to great advantage — the subject dissolves in overlapping washes that seem to have formed spontaneously on the paper. For all its apparently casual execution, the work is a compelling visual experience, evoking a precise mood of place and time.

Form dissolved in color is also the subject of *The Fire Wheel* (see page 83) of ten years later — this painting points to the complete abstraction of nature in art that Whistler was inexorably heading toward at the time of his death. One of Whistler's final statements in watercolor, *Blue and Silver: Morning, Ajaccio* (see Color Plate 17), is an extremely fresh evocation of light and atmosphere. Like most of his watercolors, it is conceived on a very small sheet of paper; but this limitation of size is transcended by the breadth of Whistler's vision as an artist.

John La Farge (1835 – 1910) has been called the most cultivated artist of his time. His French ancestry and American upbringing provided him with an international view of the world, for which he had a passionate curiosity. Painting was his first love, but he excelled at writing and lecturing as well. As an artist, his interests ranged from painting and doing murals to designing stained glass and illustrating. Throughout his long career, though, La Farge held a special regard for watercolor.

Like Whistler and so many artists of his generation, La Farge was impressed with the contemplative aspects of Oriental art. Quite early in his career, he found that painting still lifes gave him a needed opportunity for studies in contrasting textures and random arrangement of objects (see page 84). *Still Life with Chinese Vase of Roses* (see Color Plate 18), painted at the time La Farge was studying painting with William Morris Hunt, stems stylistically, from traditional European painting and does not use the compositional devices of *Japonisme* employed by Whistler. Yet the emphasis on informality and intimacy in La Farge's watercolor relates to the spirit of Oriental art, if not the form. His first direct encounter with Japanese culture was in 1886 when, in the company of the great savant of American letters, Henry Adams, he spent several months in study and travel in Japan. La Farge's writings from that time indicate a persistent tendency to relate his understanding of Japanese art and his Western heritage.

The result was not the typical tourist's delight in the picturesque, but a true assimilation of Oriental ideas. He derived his most enigmatic work, *The Strange Thing Little Kiosai Saw in the River* (see page 85), from his readings of Japanese folk tales—this painting exemplifies his most extreme use of *Japonisme*. It is a luminous watercolor of great coloristic purity, factual in its observation yet mysterious in its unexpected subject matter.

After his voyage to Tahiti and Samoa in 1890, La Farge painted many watercolors depicting his observations of the life on those exotic islands which did not differ radically in style from the rest of his painting. Unlike Paul Gauguin, who visited Tahiti at about the same time, La Farge never incorporated the brilliant colors of the island into his work. Rather, he allowed its languid charm to be expressed gently through harmonious relationships of earth tones. The slight and subtle imbalance of composition in *Bridle Path, Tahiti* (see Color Plate 19), implies a vague presence of tension and mystery. La Farge could be as forceful and direct as Homer with moments of high drama caused by nature's violence, as in *Palms in a Storm, Vaiala* (see page 86). The Tahitian watercolors are among La Farge's most lyrical works, almost in spite of his patient objectivity.

In his search for a more expressive means to convey his love of color, La Farge was attracted to the possibilities inherent in stained glass. Working with some of the most prominent architects of his time, such as H. H. Richardson, La Farge played a large part in the revival of the art of stained glass. He developed his designs, mainly for churches and public buildings, from preparatory renderings in watercolor that were often loosely sketched and have the look of spontaneous creation. *Promise of Immortality* (see page 87), a design for a stained glass window, combines La Farge's penchant for diaphanous veils of color with the monumentality of drawing. The monumentality stemmed from interpretation of Beaux-Arts neoclassical figures, a de rigueur element in the decoration of public buildings at the turn of the century.

No other period in the history of American art so comfortably wedded the talents of architect, painter, and sculptor as that era, which saw the proliferation of vast new edifices dedicated to industry, learning, and the arts. The World's Columbian Exposition, held in Chicago in 1893, called forth the talents of nearly every major figure in American art. The Exposition was viewed by the sculptor Augustus St. Gaudens as "the greatest assembly of artists since the 15th century." The radiant light of Thomas Moran's nearly mystical vision of that enterprise, *Court of Honor, Administration Building, Chicago World's Fair* (see page 88), expresses that era's nearly limitless optimism. And with its obvious allusions to the canals and palaces of Venice, the connection between Moran and Turner—who also delighted in the atmospheric effects of that city—becomes abundantly apparent.

## American Impressionism

Of the American artists who worked independently of the quasi-official academy of impressionism in New York, the Ten, Theodore Robinson (1852–96) was the most talented. He began as a student of academic realism in New York and continued in that path in Paris under C.-E. Carolus-Duran in the late 1870s. Although Robinson arrived in Paris during the year of the first impressionist exhibition, 1874, he did not begin to show a strong allegiance to impressionism until about 1886. His meeting with Claude Monet two years later confirmed that allegiance.

Robinson did not imitate either Monet's color or style of painting—he evolved a manner of his own, incorporating a number of other influences. Most of Robinson's large figure compositions of rustic maidens share the same objectivity and sentimentality of the popular Salon painters like Jules Bastien-Lepage, an academic realist whose style and subject matter place him squarely in the older Barbizon tradition. Also, Robinson frequently used photographs of the live model to paint from rather than painting from the model herself, more as a measure of economy than as an exploration of the uses of photography. While Eakins used photographs as an aid in studying human and animal locomotion and even experimented with the camera in portraiture, Robinson used the new invention as a substitute for sketching. The result was often a stiffness and artificiality.

The little watercolor *Decorative Head* (see Color Plate 21) is a detail borrowed from a much larger composition in oil, *La Vachère*, of the previous year, 1888. *Decorative Head* suggests that Robinson was really in his proper element when painting intimate pictures rather than the large Salon works expected of every aspiring artist in Paris. His landscapes attest to the same conclusion—their modest size and poetic vision permitted him to attain a level of esthetic excellence that made him a worthy companion of Monet. Robinson spent his last summer in France in Giverny, working in close association with the great master of impressionism. *A Normandy Mill* (see page 89), painted in that summer of 1892, represents Robinson as a true impressionist—it is also imbued with his highly personal idiom of muted color.

Robinson's career was cut short by a tragically early death two years later. Had he been spared, he would probably have been a major figure in the history of American art.

The one American artist at the time who most successfully assimilated the broken color and informal composition of French Impressionism was Childe Hassam (1859–1935). His first professional work was in graphics, and Hassam had a natural inclination toward drawing when he went to Europe for the first time in 1883. Upon his return to Boston that same year, he exhibited 67 of his European watercolors (see page 90) in a commercial gallery, establishing a strong claim for recognition as a serious exponent of the medium. After a protracted stay in France between 1886 and 1889, he returned to the United States as a fully accomplished impressionist painter. The success of Durand-Ruel's impressionist exhibition in New York in 1886 set the stage for both public and critical acceptance of the new style of painting. Hassam responded to this hospitable climate of critical approval; the decade of the 1890s was his most brilliant period of expression as a colorist.

Hassam divided his time between a studio in New York, in the winter months, and New England. One of his favorite painting locales was the Isle of Shoals, a few miles off the New Hampshire-Maine coast. Appledore, the principal island of the group, became a watering place for the Boston literati and was presided over by the gifted minor poet Celia Thaxter, with whom Hassam formed a lifelong friendship. A noted horticulturist, her garden was the setting for many of Hassam's paintings. *Isle of Shoals Garden* (see Color Plate 22) attains a chromatic richness of unusual brilliance—Hassam usually favored the more mellow tonalities of plein air impressionism. More characteristic of Hassam's landscape subjects in oil, *Newfields, New Hampshire* (see Color Plate 23) has a cool richness built up by bold, overlapping washes of color that deftly describe the scene in a few sure strokes. It was for this kind of painterly elegance of touch that Hassam met with such great critical and financial success during his long career. Perhaps because success came to him so easily, he did not realize the latent promise of his youthful talent. The paintings of his later years lack the power of conception and the assured technique of former days — they relapse into meager, routine performances.

## The End of Decorative Impressionism

Hassam's fate was to outlive impressionism; as a viable form of new creative effort charting new paths in art, it had been a pivot point in the swing toward modernism. But in America, where its strength was diluted by mixture with the persistent native tradition of objective realism, impressionism became absorbed in the academic establishment. By 1900, academic impressionism was the standard exhibition fare in the major national shows held regularly at the Pennsylvania Academy, the National Academy of Design, the Chicago Art Institute, the Carnegie International Exhibitions in Pittsburgh, and the Corcoran Gallery Biennials in Washington. Its devotees were to be found everywhere, offering up cheerful views of the world that contained no discordant note of the realities of urbanization, a major social phenomenon that the era of optimism—as the end of the 19th century in America has been termed—chose largely to ignore.

A number of young realist painters working in New York under the leadership of Robert Henri took a public stand on this issue in their famous group exhibition of 1908. Although most of the paintings of this so-called "Ashcan School" were pleasantly decorative works, the realism of some presented a double challenge. They questioned the integrity of the academic impressionist leadership of the art world and the whole concept of the genteel tradition in American cultural life, with its narrow, anemic estheticism.

Henri's "black gang" of realists, as they were called by some horrified art critic, did not instantly alter the course of American painting; nor did the momentous event of the New York Armory Show of 1913, which presented modern European art for the first time to the United States. The change was so gradual as to seem like evolution rather than a revolution of modernism in painting. Many able artists unsympathetic to art as social realism or theoretical modernism continued to practice decorative impressionism. Edward Potthast (1857–1927), for one, found impressionism to be his métier early in his career and pursued a lifelong devotion to it. In his youth Potthast was an illustrator, and the bulk of his work in oils is figurative. Best known for his sun-drenched beach scenes with happy bathers, Potthast is the quintessential painter of the "smiling aspects" of nature, a condition that tends to obscure his very solid contribution to landscape painting (see page 90).

Dodge MacKnight (1860–1950) was a prolific painter in watercolors. Because of his close association with Boston and an avid group of patrons in that city, however, he is not as widely recognized as he might have been had he been forced to seek a national reputation. MacKnight is perhaps the most original and emotionally expressive of the traditionalists who carried decorative impressionism well into the 20th century. His watercolors are endlessly inventive variations within a restricted color scheme of intense chromatic resonance (see Color Plate 24).

## John Singer Sargent

The three American artists who became truly international figures of the 19th-century art world—James A. McNeill Whistler, Mary Cassatt, and John Singer Sargent—are frequently termed expatriates. The implication is that they felt inhibited by the cultural climate of the United States and preferred to live and work in the more cosmopolitan environment of Europe. That was no less true of many of America's most gifted literary talents. Henry James, perhaps the most outspoken expatriate of his time, wrote extensively about that condition in his brilliant essays and novels.

John Singer Sargent (1856–1925) was not an expatriate in the strict meaning of the word; he was born in Italy of American parents (who really were expatriates) and spent the first twenty-one years of his life in Europe. He was a man of extraordinarily diverse talents: he was knowledgeable in many languages; widely read; a capable pianist with a broad command of music; and one of the most gifted portrait painters in the history of modern Western art.

Sargent was always a controversial personality. He has been disparaged as a portrait painter because he claimed to paint only what his eye could see and did not delve beneath the surface. While that is a vast oversimplification of his actual accomplishments, it is not without irony. Cézanne is reported to have said of Monet, "He is only an eye—but what an eye!" To be attacked for applying objectivity to portraiture while the same objectivity was found commendable in the landscape paintings of his old friend, Claude Monet, must have struck Sargent as ruefully humorous.

There has always been something in the propriety of his personal life—his deportment as the Edwardian gentleman-artist — that nettled his critics. Sargent lacked the colorful Bohemian swagger of Whistler, who regarded him with great hostility, calling the younger man "a sepulchre of propriety," Mary Cassatt, whose circle of friends included both the leaders of French art and members of international society, openly disliked his portraits. If Sargent was poorly regarded by these celebrated compatriots, he was reviled by the younger generation of critics who tended to denegrate any art that did not either appear to anticipate Cézanne or to emanate from him.

Sargent took up watercolor seriously at about the time he was showing signs of a deep dissatisfaction with portrait painting. Shortly after the turn of the century, he expressed a great weariness at the prospect of having to do another "pawtreet," as he put it. By 1907, he had painted some five hundred commissioned portraits as well as scores of informal ones, and his work was showing signs of becoming mechanical. In the early 1900s, Sargent learned to escape from his London studio and the demands of his clients by taking extended vacations in the Alps, Italy, or Spain. He turned to sketching in watercolor, and gradually the sketching activity blossomed into a second career as Sargent applied to it all the resources of his immense talent.

*The Shadowed Stream* (see page 91), a sensitive early statement in the medium that tells of his impressionist leanings at the time, appears to be almost the work of another artist when compared with a brio performance like *Gourds* (see Color Plate 25), made twenty years later. Sargent embarked on serious work as a landscape painter in 1885 following his move from Paris to London. There he participated in the founding of The New English Art Club, which had members that were mostly impressionists. Sargent was not attracted to the bright palette of the French plein air manner; instead, he preferred the more difficult task of painting the effects of reflected light. *Gourds* accomplishes this objective with disarming ease of execution; with only the slightest preparatory work, drawing and painting merge in one act of tour-de-force observation. This watercolor was one of more than eighty shown in 1908 at the New York galleries of M. Knoedler & Company—this exhibition established Sargent at once as a worthy

companion to Winslow Homer. Nine years later, the Carnegie Institute in Pittsburgh sponsored the first joint exhibition of Sargent and Homer watercolors. By that time, Homer was dead; as the survivor, Sargent received the tacit nomination as the foremost watercolor painter in America.

The summers between 1908 and 1914 were especially productive in watercolor paintings for Sargent as he wandered around the Mediterranean. These works speak of his elated state of mind; freed from the demands of portraiture, he launched into this "off duty" work, as he put it, with incredible zest. Any available interesting subject served his purpose. The informal study of his niece near a Swiss mountain stream, *Rose Marie Ormond Reading in a Cashmere Shawl* (see Color Plate 26), is devoid of the expected sentimentality; instead, the draped figure becomes a complicated abstract form, challenging the artist's eye and hand. The simplifications of form here are ingenious, so precisely do they assume their proper spatial relationships; yet only at some distance can the work be properly read.

Sargent's habit of choosing any subject at random and then painting it at one go was not carelessness but was rather a deliberate avoidance of easy or picturesque solutions. The snapshot quality of *Sebastiano (Man Reading)* (see page 92) or the sudden total impression of *Venetian Interior* (see page 93), seen in a passing glance, could be obtained only in this manner. Sargent often denied that he painted views—he insisted that he was only interested in objects. To a large extent that was true; his landscape subjects rarely permit the principal forms to recede very far beyond the picture plane, and apparently he did not find atmospheric effects greatly interesting. The trees in *Landscape at Frascati* (see page 94) stop the eye; satisfaction comes with the contemplation of sunlight in the foreground. Sargent's need to represent abstraction with the concrete and to confine attention to a comprehensible and small part of the world was the result of years of portrait painting. Occasionally, he would make a casual portrait in watercolor, such as the one of his sister painting in *Simplon Pass: The Lesson* (see Color Plate 27); but the subject goes beyond deft characterization to the study of contrasting values, color relationships, and the complicated play of direct and reflected light.

The war that began in Europe in 1914 ended the world of Sargent's generation. Henry James saw everything he loved "plunged into the abyss," a metaphor that seems particularly apt in considering Sargent's work in the last decade of his life. Only on his trips to the United States did he seem to recapture his ebullient flair for life. On one of these trips during the war years, Sargent visited the industrialist Charles Deering at his Florida estate. *Muddy Alligators* (see Color Plate 28), a masterful drawing enhanced by an almost iridescent color, is a performance of compelling power and awesome realism. Vizcaya, Deering's neo-Baroque palace with tropical gardens, offered Sargent countless hours of painting; his many variations on the theme *Palm Thickets* (see page 95) are among his most virtuoso performances in watercolor. The difficulties inherent in the spatial relationships of interlocking forms are compounded by formidable problems found in the patterns of light, yet Sargent seems to have relished such obstacles as interesting challenges to his command of the medium.

Sargent participated briefly in the war as an observer, commissioned by the British Imperial War Museum to create a painting that would commemorate Allied troops' cooperation in the war. While gathering notes for the project on the Western front, Sargent found time to indulge himself in an occasional watercolor. There is a detachment about all but one of them—*A Crashed Aeroplane* (see page 96)

—that tells nothing about the terrible conflict. In the sober reflection on life and death in *A Crashed Aeroplane,* though, Sargent reveals a glimpse of rare tragic feeling that is abetted by a color range of sullen beauty.

Several years later, on what would be his last visit to Boston, he called on Isabella Stewart Gardner, a friend of almost forty years. He found Mrs. Gardner, once the gayly sardonic young woman of his famous portrait, reduced by illness and infirmity to the spectre memorialized in the touching watercolor in Color Plate 29. This was a final moving tribute to a great lady, a token of respect from one survivor of the past to another.

**Trout Stream** *by George Inness, 1862. 13½" x 19¾"/34.29 x 50.16 cm. Collection of the Montclair Art Museum, Montclair, New Jersey, Photo Bill Witt.*

**Seven Boys in a Dory** *by Winslow Homer, 1873. 9½" x 13½"/24.13 x 34.29 cm. Anonymous loan.*

**The Trysting Place** *by Winslow Homer, 1875. 13¾" x 8"/34.92 x 20.32 cm.*
*Princeton University Library, Princeton, New Jersey.*

**Fisher Girl** (*also called* **The Wreck** *or* **Girl with Red Stockings)** *by Winslow Homer, 1882. 13¼" x 19-3/16"/33.66 x 48.74 cm. Courtesy Museum of Fine Arts, Boston, Massachusetts, Bequest of John T. Spaulding.*

**The Ship's Boat** *by Winslow Homer, 1883. 16" x 29"/40.64 x 73.66 cm. The New Britain Museum of American Art, New Britain, Connecticut, Charles F. Smith Fund.*

**Leaping Trout** *by Winslow Homer, c. 1889. 14" x 20"/35.56 x 50.8 cm. Courtesy Museum of Fine Arts, Boston, Massachusetts, Warren Collection, William Wilkins Warren Fund.*

**Fishing in the Adirondacks** *by Winslow Homer, c. 1890. 13⅝" x 19½"/34.61 x 49.53 cm. Courtesy of the Fogg Art Museum, Harvard University, Cambridge, Massachusetts, Louise E. Bettens Fund.*

**The Woodchopper** *by Winslow Homer, c. 1891. 14" x 20"/35.56 x 50.8 cm. Courtesy Firestone and Parsons Inc., Boston, Massachusetts.*

**Rocky Shore, Bermuda** *by Winslow Homer, 1900. 13¾" x 20"/34.92 x 50.8 cm.*
*Courtesy Museum of Fine Arts, Boston, Massachusetts, Bequest of Grenville H. Norcross.*

John Biglen (professional oarsman) in a single scull.

Thomas Eakins

**John Biglen in a Single Scull** *by Thomas Eakins, 1873 – 1874. 16¾" x 23"/42.54 x 58.42 cm. Metropolitan Museum of Art, New York, Fletcher Fund, 1924.*

**Seventy Years Ago** *by Thomas Eakins, 1877. 15⅝" x 11"/39.69 x 27.94 cm. The Art Museum, Princeton University, Princeton, New Jersey.*

**Still Life with Mandarin Oranges (Wrapped Citrus)** *by William John McCloskey,*
*1892. 8½" x 18½"/21.59 x 46.99 cm. Los Angeles County Museum of Art,*
*Los Angeles, California, lent by Mr. Steve Martin.*

**Artist Sketching in a Park** *by James Wells Champney. Watercolor and Chinese white,*
*5" x 9"/12.7 x 22.86 cm. Courtesy Museum of Fine Arts, Boston, Massachusetts,*
*M. and M. Karolik Collection.*

**The Lone Pine** *by William Keith, 1881. 14" x 10"/35.56 x 25.4 cm. Courtesy Museum of Fine Arts, Boston, Massachusetts, M. and M. Karolik Collection.*

**Portrait of a Young Woman** *by William Merritt Chase, c. 1880. 14¾" x 10⅜"/ 37.46 x 26.35 cm. Collection of Mr. and Mrs. Raymond J. Horowitz.*

**Two Boys by a Boat—Near Cape May** *by Thomas Anshutz, 1894. 13½″ x 19⅞″/33.66 x 50.48 cm. Collection of Rita and Daniel Fraad.*

**Street Scene in Ikao, Japan** *by Robert Frederick Blum, 1890. 10½″ x 12¾″/26.67 x 32.38 cm. Metropolitan Museum of Art, New York, Gift of William J. Baer, 1904.*

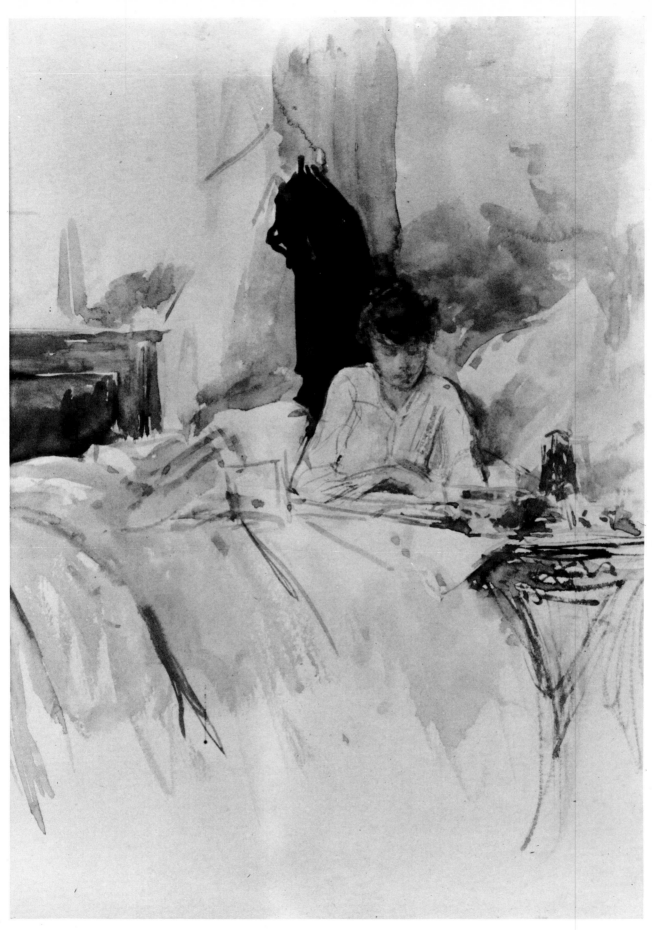

**The Artist's Model Maud Reading in Bed** *by James A. McNeill Whistler, 1886.*
*Pen and watercolor, 9⅞" x 6⅞" /25.08 x 17.46 cm. Walters Art Gallery, Baltimore,*
*Maryland.*

**The Fire Wheel** *by James A. McNeill Whistler, 1893. 3¾" x 6⅛"/9.52 x 15.56 cm.*
*University of Glasgow, Scotland, Birnie Philip Bequest.*

**Apple Blossoms** *by John La Farge. 7" x 9½"/17.78 x 24.13 cm. Courtesy Museum of Fine Arts, Boston, Massachusetts, Bequest of Mrs. H. L. Higginson.*

**The Strange Thing Little Kiosai Saw in the River** *by John La Farge, 1897. 12¾"*
*x 18½"/32.38 x 46.99 cm. Metropolitan Museum of Art, New York, Rogers Fund, 1917.*

**Palms in a Storm with Rain, Vaiala, Samoa** *by John La Farge, 1891. 18" x 11-15/16"/45.72 x 30.32 cm. The St. Louis Art Museum, St. Louis, Missouri, Eliza McMillan Fund and funds from the Estate of Edward Mallinckrodt, Sr.*

**Promise of Immortality** *by John La Farge, 7 ½" x 8"/19.05 x 20.32 cm. Courtesy Museum of Fine Arts, Boston, Massachusetts, Bequest of Elizabeth Howard Bartol.*

**Court of Honor, Administration Building, Chicago World's Fair** *by Thomas Moran, 1894. 28-3/16" x 20½"/71.6 x 52.07 cm. The Brooklyn Museum, Brooklyn, New York, Bequest of Clara L. Obrig.*

**Cliffs, Green River, Utah** *by Thomas Moran, 1872. 6-3/16" x 11-11/16"/15.72 x 29.69 cm.*
*Courtesy Museum of Fine Arts, Boston, Massachusetts, M. and M. Karolik Collection.*

**A Normandy Mill** *by Theodore Robinson, 1892. 9⅞" x 15"/25.08 x 38.1 cm.*
*Collection of Mr. and Mrs. Raymond J. Horowitz.*

**View of London** *by Childe Hassam, 1889. 7½" x 11"/19.05 x 27.94 cm. Anonymous loan.*

**An Old Dock** *by Edward H. Potthast, 1904. 22" x 30"/55.9 x 76.2 cm. The Merrill J. Gross Collection.*

**The Shadowed Stream, France** *by John Singer Sargent, c. 1885. 13½″ x 9½″/34.29 x 24.13 cm. Courtesy Museum of Fine Arts, Boston, Massachusetts, Zoe Oliver Sherman Collection.*

**Sebastiano (Man Reading)** *by John Singer Sargent, c. 1916. 13⅝" x 20¾"/34.61 x 52.7 cm. Courtesy of the Fogg Art Museum, Harvard University, Cambridge, Massachusetts, Bequest of Grenville L. Winthrop.*

**Venetian Interior** *by John Singer Sargent, c. 1910. 10" x 14"/25.4 x 35.56 cm.*
*Courtesy of the John G. Collection, Philadelphia, Pennsylvania.*

**Landscape at Frascati** *by John Singer Sargent, c. 1910. 14½″ 20½″/36.83 x 52.07 cm. Anonymous loan.*

**Palm Thicket, Vizcaya** *by John Singer Sargent, 1917. 13¾" x 21"/34.92 x 53.34 cm. Collection David Daniels, New York.*

**A Crashed Aeroplane** *by John Singer Sargent, 1918. 13½" x 21"/34.29 x 53.34 cm.*
*The Trustees of the Imperial War Museum, London.*

**Color Plate 1. Purple Grackle** *by John James Audubon, 1822. Plate 7 of* Birds of America. *23⅞" x 18½"/60.64 x 46.99 cm. Courtesy, the New York Historical Society, New York.*

**Color Plate 2. The Watercolor Class,** *anonymous, c. 1815–1820. 14⅝″ x 23⅝″/37.15 x 60.01 cm. Courtesy of The Art Institute of Chicago, Illinois.*

**Color Plate 3. Study of Ariadne** *by John Vanderlyn, 1809–1810. 4⅛" x 5½"/10.48 x 13.97 cm. Yale University Art Gallery, New Haven, Connecticut, Gift of Albro N. Dana.*

*Stony-point as you approach it from Haverstraw bay.*

**Color Plate 4. Stony Point, Haverstraw Bay, West Point** *from the* Hudson River
Sketchbook *by Charles Willson Peale, 1801. 6⅛" x 7¾"/15.56 x 19.68 cm. American
Philosophical Society, Philadelphia, Pennsylvania.*

**Color Plate 5. The Franconia Mountains from Compton, New Hampshire** *by William Trost Richards, 1872. 8-3/16" x 14-3/16"/20.8 x 36.04 cm. Metropolitan Museum of Art, New York, Gift of Reverend Elias L. Magoon.*

**Color Plate 6. At the Bridge** *by Alfred T. Bricher, 1879. Gouache, 13½" x
20¾"/34.29 x 52.7 cm. Collection Mr. Robert A. Mann.*

**Color Plate 7. Early Snow, Mt. Washington** *by Jasper F. Cropsey, 1891. 16⅛″ x
26″/40.96 x 66 cm. Wichita State University Art Collection, Wichita, Kansas, Gift of
Mr. and Mrs. Jesse A. LaDow. Also courtesy Schweitzer Gallery, New York.*

**Color Plate 8. The Mink Pond** *by Winslow Homer, 1891. 13⅞" x 20"/35.24 x 50.8 cm. Courtesy of the Fogg Art Museum, Harvard University, Cambridge, Massachusetts, Bequest of Grenville L. Winthrop.*

**Color Plate 9. Hunter in the Adirondacks** *by Winslow Homer, 1892. 13¼″ x 19½″/33.66 x 49.53 cm. Courtesy of the Fogg Art Museum, Harvard University, Cambridge, Massachusetts, Anonymous gift.*

**Color Plate 10. Sponge Fishing, Bahamas** *by Winslow Homer, c. 1899. 14" x 20"/35.56 x 50.8 cm. Canajoharie Library and Art Gallery, Canajoharie, New York.*

**Color Plate 11. Homosassa Jungle in Florida** *by Winslow Homer, 1904. 14" x 22"/35.56 x·55.9 cm. Courtesy of the Fogg Art Museum, Harvard University, Cambridge, Massachusetts, Gift of Mrs. Charles S. Homer in memory of the late Charles S. Homer and his brother Winslow Homer.*

**Color Plate 12. Diamond Shoal** *by Winslow Homer, 1905. 13½" x 21¼" /34.29 x 53.98 cm. Courtesy of the IBM Corporation.*

**Color Plate 13. Whistling for Plover** *by Thomas Eakins, 1874. 11" x 16½" /27.94 x 41.91 cm. The Brooklyn Museum, Brooklyn, New York.*

**Color Plate 14. Still Life** *by Claude Raguet Hirst, c. 1890. 10" x 14½"/25.4 x 36.83 cm. Butler Institute of American Art, Youngstown, Ohio.*

**Color Plate 15. A Concert** (*also called* **The Two Sisters**) *by Edwin Austin Abbey, 1882. 23¼" x 35½"/ 59.06 x 90.17 cm. Yale University Art Gallery, New Haven, Connecticut, The Mary Gertrude Abbey Fund.*

**Color Plate 16. The Nocturne: Grand Canal, Amsterdam** *by James A. McNeill Whistler, not later than 1884. 8-15/16" x 11-3/16"/ 22.7 x 28.42 cm. Courtesy of the Freer Gallery of Art, Smithsonian Institution, Washington, D.C.*

**Color Plate 17. Blue and Silver: Morning, Ajaccio** *by James A. McNeill Whistler,*
*c. 1901. 9⅞" x 5¾"/ 25.08 x 14.6 cm. University of Michigan Museum of Art,*
*Ann Arbor, Michigan, Bequest of Margaret Watson Parker.*

**Color Plate 18. Still Life with Chinese Vase of Roses** *by John La Farge, c. 1860.*
*16⅛" x 16"/ 40.96 x 40.64 cm. Courtesy of the Fogg Art Museum, Harvard University,*
*Cambridge, Massachusetts, Bequest of Grenville L. Winthrop.*

**Color Plate 19. Bridle Path, Tahiti** *by John La Farge, c. 1890. 18" x 20" / 45.72 x 50.8 cm. Courtesy of the Fogg Art Museum, Harvard University, Cambridge, Massachusetts, Gift of Edward D. Bettens to the Louise E. Bettens Fund.*

**Color Plate 20. Hot Springs of Gardner's River, Yellowstone, Wyoming Territory** *by Thomas Moran, 1872. 20¼" x 28⅝"/ 51.44 x 72.71 cm. Reynolda House, Inc., Museum of American Art, Winston-Salem, North Carolina.*

**Color Plate 21. Decorative Head** *by Theodore Robinson, 1889. 14" x 10"/ 35.56 x 25.4 cm. The Brooklyn Museum, Brooklyn, New York, Dick S. Ramsay Fund.*

**Color Plate 22. Isle of Shoals Garden** *by Childe Hassam, c. 1892. 19¾" x 13¾"/ 50.16 x 34.92 cm. Courtesy of National Collection of Fine Arts, Smithsonian Institution, Washington, D.C.*

**Color Plate 23. Newfields, New Hampshire** *by Childe Hassam, 1906. 13⅞" x 19⅞"/ 35.24 x 50.48 cm. The Currier Gallery of Art, Manchester, New Hampshire.*

**Color Plate 24. A Lane Through an Orange Grove, Orihuela** *by Dodge MacKnight, 1904.*
*14¾" x 21¼"/ 37.46 x 53.98 cm. Isabella Stewart Gardner Museum, Boston, Massachusetts.*

**Color Plate 25. Gourds** *by John Singer Sargent, 1905–1908. 13-12/16" x 19-11/16"/ 34.92 x 50.01 cm. The Brooklyn Museum, Brooklyn, New York.*

**Color Plate 26. Rose Marie Ormond Reading in a Cashmere Shawl** *by John Singer Sargent, c. 1908–1912. 12½" x 19½"/ 31.75 x 49.53 cm. Los Angeles County Museum of Art, Art Museum Council Fund and Anonymous Donors.*

**Color Plate 27. Simplon Pass: The Lesson** *by John Singer Sargent, 1911. 15" x 18¼"/ 38.1 x 46.36 cm. Courtesy Museum of Fine Arts, Boston, Massachusetts, Charles Henry Hayden Fund.*

**Color Plate 28. Muddy Alligators** *by John Singer Sargent, 1917. 13-9/16" x 20-15/16"/ 34.45 x 53.18 cm. Worcester Art Museum, Worcester, Massachusetts.*

**Color Plate 29. Mrs. Gardner in White** *by John Singer Sargent, September, 1922.*
*16¾″ x 12½″/ 42.54 x 31.75 cm. Isabella Stewart Gardner Museum, Boston, Massachusetts.*

**Color Plate 30. Low Tide, Beachmont** *by Maurice Prendergast, 1897. 19½" x 22⅛"/ 49.53 x 56.22 cm. Worcester Art Museum, Worcester, Massachusetts.*

**Color Plate 31. Central Park** *by Maurice Prendergast, 1901. 14⅜" x 21½"/ 36.51 x 54.61 cm. Collection of Whitney Museum of American Art, New York.*

**Color Plate 32. Screecher, Lake Rossignol** *by George B. Luks, 1919. 8⅝" x 9¼"/ 21.91 x 23.5 cm.*
*Munson-Williams-Proctor Institute Museum of Art, Utica, New York.*

**Color Plate 33. Maine Islands** *by John Marin, 1922. 16¾" x 20"/ 42.54 x 50.8 cm.*
*The Phillips Collection, Washington, D.C.*

**Color Plate 34. Storm Over Taos** *by John Marin, 1930. 15" x 20-15/16"/ 38.1 x 53.18 cm. National Gallery of Art, Washington, D.C., Alfred Stieglitz Collection.*

**Color Plate 35. Region of Brooklyn Bridge Fantasy** *by John Marin, 1932. 18¾" x 22¼"/*
*47.62 x 56.54 cm. Collection of Whitney Museum of American Art, New York.*

**Color Plate 36. Boat Movement, Cape Split** *by John Marin, 1940. 15⅜" x 20¾"/ 39.05 x 52.7 cm. Herbert F. Johnson Museum of Art, Cornell University, where the work is on extended loan from the Dr. and Mrs. Milton Lurie Kramer Collection.*

**Color Plate 37. The Circus** *by Charles Demuth, 1917. Watercolor and pencil, 8" x 10⅝"/ 20.32 x 26.99 cm. The Columbus Gallery of Fine Arts, Columbus, Ohio, Gift of Ferdinand Howald.*

**Color Plate 38. Roofs and Steeples** *by Charles Demuth, 1921. 14¼" x 10⅜"/ 36.2 x 26.35 cm. The Brooklyn Museum, Brooklyn, New York, Dick S. Ramsay Fund.*

**Color Plate 39. Eggplant and Summer Squash** *by Charles Demuth, c. 1927.*
*13½" x 19¾"/ 34.29 x 50.16 cm. Wadsworth Atheneum, Hartford, Connecticut, Ella*
*Gallup Sumner and Mary Catlin Sumner Collection.*

**Color Plate 40. Sailing by Moonlight** *by William Zorach, 1922. 21½" x 14¾"/*
*54.61 x 37.46 cm. The Phillips Collection, Washington, D.C.*

**Color Plate 41. River Rouge Industrial Plant** *by Charles Sheeler, 1928. 8" x 11¼"/ 20.32 x 28.58 cm. Museum of Art, Carnegie Institute, Pittsburgh, Pennsylvania.*

**Color Plate 42. Highland Light** *by Edward Hopper, 1930, North Truro. 15⅝" x 24½"/ 39.69 x 62.23 cm. Courtesy of the Fogg Art Museum, Harvard University, Cambridge, Massachusetts, Louise E. Bettens Fund.*

**Color Plate 43. House on Pamet River** *by Edward Hopper, 1934. 19¾" x 24⅞"/
50.16 x 63.18 cm. Collection of Whitney Museum of American Art, New York.*

**Color Plate 44. Black Horse** *by Millard Sheets, 1934. 14½" x 22"/ 36.83 x 55.9 cm.*
*Collection of Whitney Museum of American Art, New York.*

**Color Plate 45. Farm at Broad Cove, Cushing, Maine** *by Andrew Wyeth, 1941.*
*28" x 40"/ 71.12 x 101.6 cm. Portland Museum of Art, Portland, Maine, Gift of*
*Elizabeth Foster Mann in memory of Elizabeth and Maximiliam Foster, 1953.*

**Color Plate 46. Winter Solstice** *by Charles Burchfield, c. 1920–1921. 21½" x 35½"/ 54.61 x 90.17 cm. The Columbus Gallery of Fine Arts, Columbus, Ohio. Gift of Ferdinand Howald.*

**Color Plate 47. Hush Before the Storm** *by Charles Burchfield, 1947. 40" x 30"/101.6 x 76.2 cm. Courtesy of the Wichita Art Museum: The Roland P. Murdock Collection.*

**Color Plate 48. The El and Snow** *by Dong Kingman, 1946. 21" x 29⅜"/ 53.34 x 74.61 cm. Collection of Whitney Museum of American Art, New York.*

# The
# Modern
# Movement

ODERNISM came to the fore in American art within a relatively brief period; in little more than a decade after 1900, most of the early modernists had established new styles of painting that would decide the course of future trends. By that year, Robert Henri had established an art school in New York where he attracted a number of young painters, many of whom had been artist-illustrators for metropolitan newspapers. As such, they brought a realism to their paintings that was taken from the ordinary life of the cities in which they lived.

## Early Modernists

One such artist who brought realism to his paintings was William Glackens (1870–1938) — his lively and dramatic watercolors of the war in Cuba, where he served as a correspondent for *McClure's Magazine*, earned him wide recognition (see page 153). In 1908, Glackens participated in the landmark exhibition of The Eight American Painters in New York along with Maurice Prendergast (1859–1924), whose decorative, impressionist style contrasted sharply with the realist manner of the majority of the artists who composed The Eight.

Prendergast was not part of the academic impressionist establishment, however, for he embraced a concept of painting that appealed primarily to the eye, with a kind of physical language not concerned with realism. His early works resemble the poetic tonalist painting of Whistler, but by the 1890s Prendergast had already evolved his own distinctive mannerisms. *Low Tide, Beachmont* (see Color Plate 30), typical of the New England beach scenes he loved, is couched in terms that show the parallel course his art was taking in relation to French post-impressionism, although he was not aware of the similarities in his work at the time. In 1898, Prendergast went to Europe and saw Cézanne's work for the first time. The experience confirmed the direction he had taken instinctively — to invest his paintings with the poetry of color, made vital through the play of sensuous surface pattern. His Venetian watercolors (see page 154) obtained a new richness and range of color while losing none of the delicacy of handling.

Prendergast's pictures have been described as tapestries of color, an idea that is exemplified in the flat, two-dimensional quality of *Central Park* (see Color Plate 31), where the color is organized into insistent horizontal bands of pattern. And while his work did not aim at approximating the effects of light and atmosphere, there are occasional essays into naturalism — *April Snow, Salem* (see page 155), with its play of colorful forms against white departs from an impressionist naturalism mainly in point of technique. Prendergast's manner of painting was uniquely his own. Perhaps the allusion to tapestry is not accurate enough to describe it; rather, his pictures are made of carefully isolated and liquid color notes that resemble the enamel colors of cloisonné,

arranged in interlocking patterns of subtle complexity. From about 1915, Prendergast worked mainly in oils, carrying forward the innovations of style he had established earlier in the watercolor medium.

Arthur B. Davies (1862–1928) is as well known for his efforts as an impresario of modernism in American art as he is for his paintings. Davies was instrumental in organizing The Eight exhibition of 1908 and the International Exhibition of Modern Art — known popularly as The Armory Show—of 1913. In spite of his progressive attitudes, his lyrical figure paintings are only tinged with a modernism that seems merely applied rather than an integral part of his compositions. Davies was at his best in the spontaneous landscape paintings for which he had a genuinely poetic feeling. *From the Quai d'Orleans* (see page 156), a work of his last years, speaks of a talent fully in command of the expressive means of the watercolor medium.

Another member of The Eight, George Luks (1867–1933), painted more in the social realist vein of Henri's group, adopting a manner based on his admiration for the portraits of Frans Hals. Luks' visceral approach to oil painting has tended to overshadow an important aspect of his art, his work in watercolor. Those accustomed to the heavy impasto and dark tonalities of his oils find Luks' quite different work in watercolor delightfully out of character. In his watercolors, Luks adopted an almost Fauvist colorism, the bright harmonies reflecting his enjoyment of nature while on vacation and away from the preoccupations with city life. Nova Scotia, the setting for the Lake Rossignol picture (see Color Plate 32), inspired some of the most boldly inventive color statements by any American artist of the period.

George O. Hart (1868–1953), known as "Pop" Hart to a younger generation of painters, extended the social realism of Henri's group beyond the confines of New York to distant places. The Caribbean and Mexico were strong catalysts; he delighted in scenes of native life and worked with an easy, fluid touch that is superficially masked by his pervasively humorous treatment of subject matter (see page 157).

Foremost among the American modernists of his generation, John Marin (1870–1953) made the largest contribution to watercolor painting in this century. In his command of the medium, he ranks with Winslow Homer. Creating his art out of a love of the forms and moods of nature, Marin, like Homer, was carrying on the symbiotic relationship between the artist and the land that had persisted in American art throughout the 19th century. In even his most aggressively abstract compositions, Marin retained reference points to nature, if only in the place names of the individual paintings.

Marin was almost thirty before he turned from an apprenticeship in architecture to a brief period of formal study of art. He passed quickly through the Pennsylvania Academy of the Fine Arts and the Art Students League in New York and with no further training went to Europe in 1905, the year of the

Fauve exhibition at the Salon d'Automne in Paris. The modern movement took hold of him almost immediately; his first serious work in Europe was in the medium of etching, and later, watercolor.

In 1909, the avant-garde art dealer and photographer Alfred Steiglitz gave Marin a small exhibition in his Photo-Secession Gallery on Fifth Avenue, New York. Marin's return to the United States in 1911 was followed by an outpouring of work in watercolor celebrating the vitality of urban life. He was greatly impressed by the burgeoning new architecture of New York: ". . . if those buildings move me they too must have life. Thus the whole city is alive, the buildings, the people, are all alive; and the more they move me the more I feel them to be alive." The Cubist idiom of *Movement, Fifth Avenue* (see page 158) was the inevitable and logical choice for the expression of those ideas—Marin's espousal of cubist-expressionist manners in art was a matter of conviction, though, not of fashion.

In 1914, Marin visited Maine for the first time, beginning what would be a lifelong communion with the spirit of rock and wave. He desired to distill the essence of life that he saw in the forms of those substances, much as he had perceived the underlying motive power of New York architecture. His art was a more overtly emotional response to nature than was that of Winslow Homer, yet the two shared a common belief in the importance of the meanings to be found in elemental things.

The crystalline geometry of *Maine Islands* (see Color Plate 33) is conceived in terms of symbols that Marin invented to express the idea—not the illusion—of space. He saw the elements of the physical world ". . . at work, pushing, pulling, sideways, downwards, upwards. I can hear the sound of their strife and there is great music being played." The forms of *Mt. Chocorua* (see page 159), simply and powerfully stated, are as convincing in their symbolism as those in the representational idiom of Thomas Cole, who painted the same subject a hundred years before Marin. Marin was always supremely conscious of the need to separate the image from reality. *Pertaining to Stonington Harbor, Maine, No. 4* (see page 160) insists by its very title that the viewer thinks of essences of spirit, not of material substance; the term "pertaining to" is a necessary addition to most of Marin's work.

Marin visited New Mexico in 1929 in order to shake himself free of the danger—as he saw it—of becoming confined to, and perhaps the prisoner of, mannerisms associated with painting variations on a few familiar themes. The stark and beautiful desert country around Taos, punctuated by the vigorous forms of the surrounding mountains, offered new prospects of exhilarating novelty. *Storm over Taos* (see Color Plate 34) was not only an abrupt change from his previous style, which tended to enclose space, but it also signaled a new dramatic colorism in his work. Back home in New York and Maine, Marin embarked with renewed vigor on restatements of earlier themes. *Region of Brooklyn Bridge Fantasy* (see

Color Plate 35) possesses that lusty quality he applied to the aggressive handling of the brush and to his forceful color relationships.

Marin's definitive statements, in both oil and watercolor, are products of an intimate communion with nature. This is particularly true of the watercolors he created at Cape Split, Maine, which became Marin's summer residence for the last twenty years of his life. Wave forms took on an almost violent animation as he described the sea as a living organism in one work after another (see page 161). The dynamics of form within a composition like *Boat Movement, Cape Split* (see Color Plate 36) generate a life of their own, suggesting powerful action. However removed from representational art his work may be, Marin always regarded himself as a realist responding to nature: "The sea that I paint may not be *the* sea, but it is *a* sea, not an abstraction."

Although Marin may have been the first American to paint a purely abstract picture as early as 1903–04 (and there is some question about his claim to this achievement), Arthur Dove (1880–1946) established that mode of painting as a fixed style in 1910—and he rarely wavered from it thereafter. Dove's mature efforts, like Marin's, came after he was thirty and followed a period of study abroad during which time he came to admire the daring color of the Fauve painters. A man of great wit and sensibility, he saw nature as a constantly changing yet wonderfully integrated whole, possessing forms and colors the motifs of which could be expressed symbolically in art (see page 162). Dove's watercolors tend to be spontaneous expressions, given over to a free flow of inventive color and form that evoke a quality of playfulness and humor not usually associated with abstraction. Closely related to Dove's work, the early watercolors of Georgia O'Keeffe (1887–    ) are lyrical abstractions of natural forms. In a series of watercolors, of which *Blue No. II* (see page 163), is a part, O'Keeffe drew her inspiration from the simplifications and quiet harmonies of Oriental painting—those of the Japanese and Chinese classical traditions—rather than from modern European sources. These remarkable papers enunciated O'Keeffe's lifelong involvement with the interpretation of the organic forms of nature. Both O'Keeffe and Stuart Davis (1894–1964) are best known for their paintings in oil; Davis' excursions into watercolor were restricted mainly to studies he made in gouache for larger paintings. *Iris* (see page 164), a coolly conceived and elegant cubist arrangement, prefigures his famous *Eggbeater* series of oil paintings of 1928. *Iris* reflects Davis' determined efforts to depart from the confines of his previous representational style and to seek solutions to the picture-making process through more advanced means based on the post-cubist work of Léger and Picasso.

Charles Demuth (1883–1935), reflecting on his career in relation to another master of watercolor, once remarked: "John Marin and I draw our inspiration from the same source, French Modernism. He brought his up in buckets and spilt much along the way. I dipped mine out with a teaspoon, but I never spilled a drop." Demuth was an esthete, and his paintings and watercolors exude a refinement that occasionally borders on the precious. But the sheer brilliance of his command of watercolor techniques saves his best work from becoming effete.

Unlike Marin, Demuth was accomplished in figure drawing and made it central in his work. For his own amusement he frequently turned to making watercolor illustrations of his favorite novels, such as Henry James' *Turn of the Screw* and Emile Zola's *Nana*. In flamboyant compositions like *The Circus* (see Color Plate 37), he exulted in playfully expressive drawing, reinforced by an exquisite color sense.

At the same period in his career, Demuth alternated between the organic forms of his figurative works and a highly personal treatment of Cubist form. *Roofs and Steeples* (see Color Plate 38) owes much to his 1912–14 residence in Paris and to his close association with Marcel Duchamp, who had electrified the American art world in 1913 with his *Nude Descending the Staircase,* the most controversial painting exhibited in The Armory Show. Demuth's essential fastidiousness and elegance is ultimately best employed on those little miracles of still life painting that are unique in American art. Although expressing a debt to the master Cézanne, they transcend any formal analysis of stlye. His flower subjects, painted with those veils of floating pigment peculiar to his watercolors alone, reproduce the delicacy of fragile petals (see pages 165 and 166). And the resonant depth of color of *Egg Plant and Summer Squash* (see Color Plate 39) evokes a palpable realism of the subject. But these extraordinary performances are not, after all, trompe l'oeil images—Demuth's art is not illusionary but evocative.

## American Cubism

Cubism emerged fully formed from the studios of Picasso and Braque in 1908; but once the various permutations of analytical cubism were exhausted, painters were free to apply its principles in more individualistic statements. Among American artists there was a distinct tendency to infuse a romantic syntax into the rather austere pictorial grammar of the new style. Preston Dickinson (1891–1930) had been a student in Paris in the years immediately following the first public showing of cubist art. In his work thereafter, he sought a synthesis of the new language of art with a traditional regard for the inherent poetry of landscape painting (see page 167).

While form dominated Dickinson's paintings, the color of the post-impressionist and Fauve painters stood out in the work of William Zorach (1887–1966). During the years 1911–22, before he turned to sculpture, Zorach produced some of the most lyrical statements in watercolor of any artist of his generation (see Color Plate 40).

An older artist who did not reach his mature style of painting until he was nearly forty, Max Weber (1881–1961) centered his work in an expressionist idiom after much searching through eclectic styles derived from Cézanne to Picasso. His figures, especially, convey a rich emotional response to his Jewish religious and ethnic background (see page 168). Weber's art is related to the School of Paris in its preference for expressionist form, although his Russian origins gave his work a more international orientation.

A purely American variant of cubism appeared in the 1920s. It had none of the lyrical color of Dove's inventions, nor the emotionally expressive power of Marin's work; rather, it conveyed a sturdy conviction about the significance of material things that was distinctly American. The movement has been called "Immaculate" and "Precisionist"; but regardless of the terminology, it found a rich source of visual stimuli in the forms of industrial and urban America. Charles Sheeler (1883–1965), the foremost exponent of precisionism, combined photography and painting in one career. For Sheeler photography offered a ". . . possibility of accounting for the visual world with an exactitude not equaled by any other medium." However, Sheeler's vision was far more penetrating than photographic presentation. Even in paintings based on photographic aids, Sheeler selected his subjects with great perception and feeling for their symbolic values. His spare, taut still life compositions of the twenties were manifestations of his preference for logic and simplification in art (see page 169). These preferences were reflected in his choice of Shaker architecture and furniture both in his life-style and in his paintings.

The precisionist movement also found a beauty of form in the geometry of industrial architecture that was strictly modern in its cubist implications, although it was still capable of embodying the traditional realist persuasion of American art. In *River Rouge Industrial Plant* (see Color Plate 41), a watercolor study for a larger version of the same subject in oils, Sheeler transferred his objective vision in landscape painting from an interest in organic forms to man-made shapes, symbolizing the shift in emphasis from rural to urban life in the 20th century.

## Romantic Realism

The major exponent of romantic realism in the first half of this century was Edward Hopper (1882–1967). Like Winslow Homer, with whom he is often compared, Hopper devoted a large part of his productive career to watercolor painting, and made it as significant in his total oeuvre as his work in oils. His earliest attempts in watercolor were figure pieces, resembling the graphic realism of The Eight, for he had come briefly under the influence of Robert Henri in New York. Many of these figurative works were products of his three trips to Paris between 1906 and 1910, and serve to demonstrate how unaffected he was by the great upheavals brought on by the fauve and cubist exhibitions during that period. Hopper exhibited in The Armory Show of 1913 and sold only one work; it would be another decade before he found another client for his art. Discouraged, he retreated into commercial illustration during those lean years, and gained some recognition as an etcher. About 1923 Hopper commenced serious work in watercolor, and with a highly successful exhibition in New York during the following year his career began to prosper. There is very little change in style to be noticed in Hopper's watercolors during the twenty years from 1924—a period that marks his most prolific activity with the medium. Always strongly attracted to the eclectic architecture of the American scene, Hopper's mansarded mansions like *Haskell's House* evoke a powerful nostalgia. Even on his painting trips away from New England, Hopper's imagination fastened on ideas of solitude and isolation. *St. Francis Towers, Santa Fe* (see page 170) records no human presence, as if it were a ghost town rather than the lively artist colony it had already become by 1925.

*House of the Fog Horn* (see page 171), with its squat architecture caught in the force of the wind seems to hug the earth, while *Highland Light, North Truro* (see Color Plate 42) tells of the stolid resistance of the sentinel tower to the elements of wind and sea. In such icons of New England culture Hopper's love of his subjects causes him to anthropomorphize the inanimate. Light falling on forms, with the play of cast shadows and reflections achieves more than mere description in Hopper's watercolors; there is a simplification of form in even his most insistently representational pictures that, at their core, suggest the influence of cubism. This tendency is completely realized in *House on Pamet River* (see Color Plate 43).

Hopper was a most facile technician in the handling of watercolor. He painted in a very orthodox manner, employing overlapping glazes and strictly avoiding the use of opaque white for highlight effects. His early watercolors were directly painted from nature, usually in one sitting. Eventually, as he came to see his watercolors as major creative efforts, he began to apply a studio method to their production. Later pictures like *White River at Sharon* (see page 172), have none of the occasional accidents one sees in earlier watercolors. The consequent tightening of pictorial space and the reduction to the essential elements within the composition of *Cobb's House* (see page 173), mark it as one of the ultimate refinements of his watercolor work. Hopper tended to defy the changing conventions in American art, to remain centered on a tradition of painting that, in lesser hands, became merely old-fashioned. In the face of the onrushing abstract expressionist painting of the 40s and early 50s, his work remained deeply personal, yet vital; its meaning profoundly rooted in ideas about man's loneliness, Hopper's art retains an enduring humanist orientation.

## Academic Impressionism

Particularly in the 20th century, watercolor painting has attracted artists known for the brilliance of their technical mastery of the medium. Generally, the conservative painters have demonstrated a more rigorous adherence to traditional means. By using overlapping washes of transparent color, with highlights achieved from the white paper alone, they structured the painting into a logical, orderly pictorial space by means of knowledgeable, accurate drawing. Creating a palpable realism through such a demanding medium as watercolor has worked as a challenge to artists. Sargent was the first major artist to regard watercolor as an extension of oil painting, in which brushwork and drawing become fused in one act. While he was anything but a purist about technique, Sargent demonstrated the importance of color and value relationships, mastery of drawing, and spontaneity in accomplishing both. In terms of representational art, Sargent set the standard by which all subsequent painters in watercolor were guided. The Boston portrait painter, Frank W. Benson (1862 – 1951), was one of the Ten American Painters group whose style of academic impressionism was indebted to Sargent. Like Sargent, Benson found in watercolor a medium for the kind of spirited sketching that he did not practice in the studio. Especially in his scenes of the sporting life he enjoyed, Benson transmits a buoyancy and enjoyment, both of his subjects and of the act of painting (see page 174). *Bald Eagles in Winter* (see page 175), attains the kind of elegant composition and dramatic contrasts that one finds in similar subjects by Audubon, but Benson enlivens his performance with brilliant, slashing brushwork. John Whorf (1903–1959) continued the painting tradition of Sargent and Benson. Primarily a painter in watercolors, his preference for marine subjects obscured his considerable gifts for landscape views, which, like *New England Coastal Scene* (see page 176), show him thoroughly adept at the academic impressionist mode. Ogden Pleissner (1905 –       ) combines a romantic realist point of view with an extremely incisive manner of handling the medium. An inveterate traveler, Pleissner paints with a kind of photojournalist's selectivity, as in *The Shrine* (see page 177) where a small section of wall takes on an unexpected drama through the dynamics of design and rich color patterns. Like Pleissner, Millard Sheets (1907 –       ) has become one of the most popular of our watercolor painters, admired as much for his superb handling of the medium as he is for his delightfully inventive subjects (see Color Plate 44). Although Andrew Wyeth (1917 –       ) has restricted his recent work in watercolor to small drybrush studies for larger paintings in tempera, he formerly preferred watercolor as a medium for final statements. *Farm at Broad Cove* (see Color Plate 45) is one of the largest and most completely realized papers he has produced. It appeared at a time when his very different, fluid style was changing in the direction of his now familiar manner of tight drawing and careful application of color.

## Social Realism

Occupying a position midway between academic realism and expressionism, Reginald Marsh (1898 –

1954) incorporated in his watercolors a lively, sinuous draftsmanship with only a modicum of interest in color. His concern was for the expressive meaning found in modeled form. Marsh described the human condition in terms that relate his work to that of the social realists of the turn of the century (see pages 178-179). Color, on the other hand, is realized in the work of Isabel Bishop (1902–    ) with an exquisite delicacy, applied in the manner of a thin veil, gently blurring the underlying humanist orientation of her art (see page 180). That these two artists should be preoccupied with very similar aspects of urban life and arrive at such disparate pictorial solutions is evidence of the diversity to be found in American art in the period just prior to the Second World War. Many European artists emigrated to the United States during that period in order to escape the censorship of their native countries or the dislocations brought on by the chaos of war. Their arrival in this country subtly influenced the directions of American art, especially in the area of expressionist and surrealist painting. George Grosz (1893–1959) brought a new perception to the idea of social realism; his "landscapes of the mind" are at once surrealist fantasies and satirical commentaries on the depravity of the human spirit, as he saw it (see page 181). In a more astringent vein, Lyonel Feininger (1871–1956) related the developments of modern German art to the American precisionist tradition. Feininger had gone to Europe at sixteen, and in 1937 he returned as a distinguished artist who occupied a central position in modern art. His muted color and delicate crystalline style of drawing were ideally suited to application in watercolor (see page 182), and his artistic vision inadvertently reiterated the parallel manner of American precisionists like Charles Sheeler.

## Individualism

Charles E. Burchfield (1893–1967) emerged out of the heartland of America as a kind of innocent genius who, in virtual isolation, had formed a highly personal style of painting without having been exposed to any strong influences, either from Europe or from the example of his compatriots. An astonishingly prolific painter, his entire output was very nearly confined exclusively to the watercolor medium. Early in his career, Burchfield devised his own iconography of form which he called "conventions for abstract thought." These were symbols based on expressions of the human face with which he invested a human spirit in the trees, houses, and woodland forms of his pictures. As such, Burchfield was a primitive artist—which he acknowledged—but his native ability enabled him to express himself in lyrical color and lively drawing that raises his work far beyond the usual limitations of the self-taught artist. Early evidence of his success at simplification of natural forms, *Noontide in Late May* (see page 183) is also a curiously convincing evocation of light through simple emphasis of color patterns. Always attuned to the changing moods of nature, Burch-

field could summon up on paper the dismal dampness of a winter thaw in *Winter Solstice* (see Color Plate 46). The painting epitomizes his instinctive reaching for the static verticals, the blankly staring houses, and the sentinel trees to express the special lassitude of that moment in time.

During the 30s, Burchfield turned to working in a manner of a blandly descriptive realism, painting industrial forms that evidently did not satisfy him. He soon returned to the organic shapes with which his art described the fantasies of his dream world. The gingerbread architecture of rural America ideally complemented Burchfield's interest in representing nature in a somewhat baroque manifestation. Many of his best compositions, like *Lavender and Old Lace* (see page 184) seem fraught with apprehension, a quality admirably caught also in *Hush Before the Storm* (see Color Plate 47). Burchfield believed that, "An artist must paint not what he sees in nature, but what is there. To do so, he must invent symbols, which, if properly used, make his work seem even more real than what is in front of him." The reality of what he called the "there" in nature occasionally generated images of truly cataclysmic import. Of *Sun and Rocks* (see page 185) the artist said it was ". . . a scene in primeval times, when conflicting forces of nature hold sway and seem to fill the earth with violence and chaos." Burchfield stands as one of the most eloquent artists of modern times, one who worked at rejuvenating the tradition of a spiritual bond between humanity and nature.

## Regionalism and Social Commentary

By mid-century, expressionism had thoroughly penetrated American art and had become a vehicle for expressions of purely regional and ethnic themes. Thomas Hart Benton (1889–1975) studied cubism in Europe but found the formalism of its esthetic less meaningful to him than the impress of American history, an inheritance from his family's traditions in Missouri history, and his admiration for the paintings of another Missouri artist, the 19th-century genre painter, George Caleb Bingham. His passionate devotion to the scenes of his middle western environment generated an impressive oeuvre, both mural paintings and easel pictures, making Benton the leading exponent of regionalism in the United States. He eschewed literal description in favor of a modified expressionist approach to painting, blending sinuous line and sometimes strident color with homely observations of rural life or fiercely nationalistic renditions of American history (see page 186). Benton's occasional excursions into watercolor painting produced a number of brilliant papers. Charming in conception and fresh in color, they are always distinguished performances that make one wish he had devoted more of his vast energies in that direction. In looking at the paintings of Ben Shahn (1898–1969) one might label this artist a regionalist also, but with the distinction that Shahn's province was the geography of urban social issues. An intensely political creature, he came to prominence in the early 30s with a series of gouache paintings dealing with the notorious Sacco-Vanzetti trial. Shahn continued to make trenchant pictorial commentary until the end of his life, observing everything from the foibles of humanity in works like *Existentialists* (see page 187) to the Damoclean sword of nuclear warfare. The style of his work is characterized by bold, flattened forms and rich color that respects the idea of the integrity of the painting surface and avoids any digression into naturalism. This is the manner also of Jacob Lawrence (1917–　) a Black artist who has always been motivated by the analogous social problems of his race. Describing his work, Lawrence observed, "I was always inspired by the Black esthetic . . . motivated to manipulate form, color, space, line and texture to depict our life and stimulated by the beauty and poignancy of our environment." His paintings are conceived in terms of poster art, the figurative elements presented as cutouts dramatizing the harshness of Black ghetto life (see page 188). In quite a different mode, the watercolors of Dong Kingman (1911–　) also reveal strong racial influences. Kingman, born in California of Oriental ancestry, paints his cityscapes in a highly decorative and gayly colorful manner. His handling of complicated patterns of color and form is at once boldly contemporary in feeling and yet ingratiatingly gentle, revealing a synthesis of cultural influences (see Color Plate 48).

## Abstract Expressionism

Given the limitations of the watercolor medium, it was not employed generally by the leaders of the abstract expressionist movement of the 40s and early 50s. They demanded of paint a more powerful physical presence to convey their intensely individualistic and sometimes exhibitionistic performances. In conclusion, those artists whose quietism is expressed through the subtleties of watercolor will bring this survey to a close. Mark Tobey (1890–1976) was principally a figurative painter until about 1940, but even during the 30s he began moving in the direction of total abstraction. His interest in Oriental calligraphy was an inevitable development of a contemplative turn of mind that saw in automatic writing a means to express the deeply imbedded emotions of the spirit. The "white writing" of his most characteristic paintings was the result, creating a new vision of a wholly subconscious world based on linear patterns that seem to float endlessly through the limitless spaces of the artist's mind (see page 189). Morris Graves (1910–　) came under the

same Oriental influences at about the same time as Tobey and was briefly his student. However, Graves was much more specifically attuned to Zen Buddhist philosophy, a circumstance that probably kept his work aligned in a more orthodox way to the traditions of Chinese and Japanese scroll painting. His bird and animal subjects are charged with a pervasive pathos that have a profound mysticism (see page 190). Similar intimations of the mysterious darknesses hiding in the human spirit can be found in the paintings of Mark Rothko (1903-70) of the 40s. His surrealist images, inspired by primitive myth and ritual, were created shortly before he turned to the completely abstract fields of color which were Rothko's ultimate statements as an artist (see page 191).

While the art of landscape painting may seem antithetical to the uses of modernism, a few contemporary painters have successfully assimilated a preference for nature with methods that relate their work to the present. William Thon (1906–　) accommodates colors and forms of rock and tree motifs to a two-dimensional picture plane without losing either the desired flatness of a purely abstract composition or the textures of nature (see page 192). Working almost exclusively in watercolor, Thon is one of the major practitioners in the medium to carry on in the great tradition of past artists who found nourishment for their art in the austere Maine landscape. William Kienbusch (1914–　) has evolved a highly personal style of abstract expressionism, while keeping almost exclusively within the various aqueous media of tempera, gouache, and watercolor. His long association with Maine and the New England coast and his deep feeling for the art of his illustrious predecessors in that region has endowed his work with a profound response to the special ambience of place (see page 193). Like Marin, Kienbusch has rooted his art in the spirit of nature rather than in surface appearances, and carries forward into our own time the impulse of the American artist to celebrate what Thomas Cole meant when he wrote over a hundred years ago:

".  .  . whether he beholds the Hudson mingling waters with the Atlantic, explores the central wilds of this vast continent, or stands on the margin of the distant Oregon, [the American] is still in the midst of American scenery — it is his own land; its beauty, its sublimity, all are his; and how undeserving of such a birthright if he can turn toward it an unobserving eye, an unaffected heart!"

**Raising the Flag over the Royal Palace in Santiago on July 17th, 1898** *by William Glackens, 1898. 25" x 16¾"/63.5 x 42.54 cm. Courtesy of Library of Congress, Wash. D.C.*

**Piazza de San Marco** *by Maurice Prendergast, c. 1898. 16⅛″ x 15″/40.96 x 38.1 cm.*
*Metropolitan Museum of Art, New York, Gift of the Estate of Mrs. Edward*
*Robinson, 1952.*

**April Snow, Salem** *by Maurice Prendergast, 1906–1907. 14¾" x 21⅝"/37.46 x 54.93 cm. Collection, The Museum of Modern Art, New York, Gift of Abby Aldrich Rockefeller.*

**From the Quai d'Orleans** *by Arthur B. Davies, 1925. 10-9/16" x 14-9/16"/26.83 x 36.99 cm. The Brooklyn Museum, Brooklyn, New York, Gift of the Artist.*

**The Bahamas** *by George O. Hart, c. 1918. 13 ½" x 21 ½"/34.29 x 54.61 cm.*
*Collection of the Whitney Museum of American Art, New York.*

**Movement, Fifth Avenue** *by John Marin, 1912. 16⅝″ x 13½″/42.23 x 34.29 cm.*
*Courtesy of The Art Institute of Chicago, Alfred Stieglitz Collection.*

**Mt. Chocorua** *by John Marin, 1926. 17¼" x 22"/43.82 x 55.9 cm. Courtesy of the Fogg Art Museum, Harvard University, Cambridge, Massachusetts, Pritchard Fund.*

**Pertaining to Stonington Harbor, Maine, No. 4** *by John Marin, 1926. 15⅝" x 21¾"/39.69 x 55.24 cm. Metropolitan Museum of Art, New York, Alfred Stieglitz Collection, 1949.*

**Cape Split** *by John Marin, 1939–1942. 22" x 28"/55.9 x 71.12 cm. Wichita Art Museum: The Roland P. Murdock Collection, Wichita, Kansas.*

**The Hand Sewing Machine** *by Arthur Dove, 1944. 7" x 5"/18 x 13 cm. Herbert F. Johnson Museum of Art, Cornell University, Gift of Mr. and Mrs. Morris G. Bishop.*

**Blue No. II** *by Georgia O'Keefe. 15⅞ x 10 15/16/40.32 x 27.8 cm. The Brooklyn Museum, Brooklyn, New York, Bequest of Miss Mary T. Cockcroft.*

**Iris** *by Stuart Davis, 1947. Gouache, 14⅝" x 18¼"/37.15 x 46.36 cm. Metropolitan Museum of Art, New York, George A. Hearn Fund, 1948.*

**Lily** *by Charles Demuth, 1923. 22⅞" x 17"/58.12 x 43.18 cm. Courtesy of the Fogg Art Museum, Harvard University, Cambridge, Massachusetts, Gift of Friends of the Fogg Art Museum.*

**Poppies** *by Charles Demuth, 1926. 19½" x 13⅝"/49.53 x 34.61 cm. Santa Barbara Museum of Art, California, Gift of Wright Ludington.*

**Hillside** *by Preston Dickinson, 1919. 16¾" x 11-3/16"/42.54 x 28.42 cm. The Columbus Gallery of Fine Arts, Columbus, Ohio, Gift of Ferdinand Howald.*

**Summer** *by Max Weber, 1911. Gouache on cardboard, 24⅛" x 18½"/61.3 x 47 cm.*
*Collection of Whitney Museum of American Art, New York.*

**Classic Still Life** *by Charles Sheeler, 1947. Tempera, 15 ½" x 12 ½"/31.75 x 39.37 cm. The Roy R. Neuberger Museum, State University of New York, College at Purchase, New York.*

**St. Francis Towers, Santa Fe, New Mexico** *by Edward Hopper, 1925. 13½" x 19½"/34.29 x 49.53 cm. The Phillips Collection, Washington, D.C.*

**House of the Fog Horn** *by Edward Hopper, 1927. 12½″ x 19½″/31.75 x 49.53 cm.*
*Metropolitan Museum of Art, New York, Bequest of Elizabeth Amis Cameron*
*Blanchard, 1956.*

**White River at Sharon** *by Edward Hopper, 1937. 19⅜" x 27⅜"/33.97 x 69.53 cm.*
*Sara Roby Foundation Collection, New York.*

**Cobb's House, South Truro** *by Edward Hopper, 1942. 21½" x 29½"/54.61 x 74.93 cm. Worcester Art Museum, Worcester, Massachusetts, Gift of Stephen C. Clark.*

**The Fisherman** *by Frank W. Benson, 1922. 19½″ x 15½″/49.53 x 39.37 cm. Anonymous loan.*

**Bald Eagles in Winter** *by Frank W. Benson, 1930. 29¾" x 22"/75.56 x 55.9 cm.*
*Courtesy of Childs Gallery, Boston, Massachusetts.*

**New England Coastal Scene** *by John Whorf. 14⅝" x 21¼"/37.15 x 53.98 cm.*
*Hirschl and Adler Galleries, New York.*

**The Shrine** *by Ogden Minton Pleissner. 21" x 31"/53.34 x 78.74 cm. Metropolitan Museum of Art, New York, Hugo Kastor Fund, 1962.*

**New Dodgem** *by Reginald Marsh, 1940. 40¼" x 26¾"/102.24 x 68 cm. Collection of Whitney Museum of American Art, New York, Anonymous gift.*

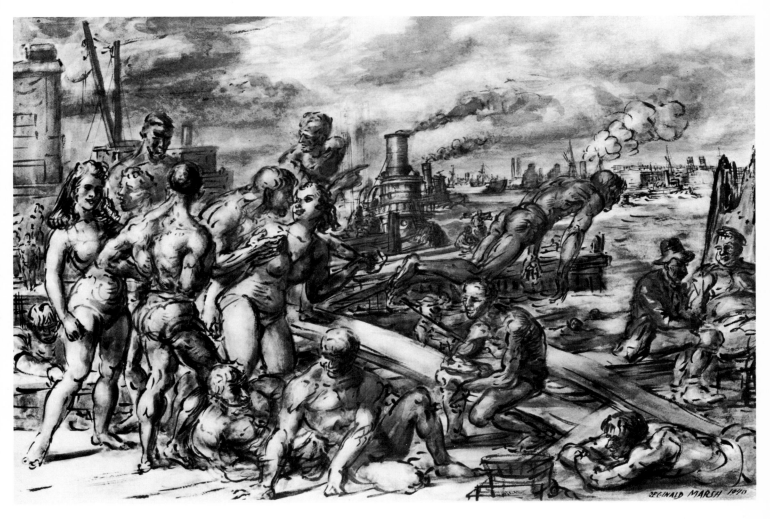

**Swimming off West Washington Market** *by Reginald Marsh, 1940. 26¾" x 40¼"/67.9 x 102.24 cm. Albright-Knox Art Gallery, Buffalo, New York, Room of Contemporary Art Fund.*

**Card Game** *by Isabel Bishop, c. 1942. 17⅞" x 18⅞"/45.40 x 47.94 cm. The Brooklyn Museum, Brooklyn, New York, Henry. L. Batterman Fund.*

**Couple** *by George Grosz, 1934. 25¼" x 17¾"/64.14 x 45.08 cm. Collection of the Whitney Museum of American Art, New York.*

**The River** *by Lyonel Feininger, 1940. 13" x 20"/33.02 x 50.8 cm. Worcester Art Museum, Worcester, Massachusetts.*

**Noontide in Late May** *by Charles Burchfield, 1917. Watercolor and gouache, 21⅝" x 17½"/ 54.93 x 44.45 cm. Collection of the Whitney Museum of American Art, New York.*

**Lavender and Old Lace** *by Charles Burchfield, 1939–1947. 37"/93.98 x 127 cm. The New Britain Museum of American Art, New Britain, Connecticut, Charles F. Smith Fund.*

**Sun and Rocks** *by Charles Burchfield, 1918-1950. 40" x 56"/101.6 x 142.24 cm.*
*Albright-Knox Art Gallery, Buffalo, New York, Room of Contemporary Art Fund.*

**Spring Tryout** *by Thomas Hart Benton, 1944. 26" x 34"/66 x 86.36 cm. Collection of Mr. and Mrs. Phillip Grace.*

**Existentialists** *by Ben Shahn, 1957. 38⅝" x 25⅝"/98.11 x 65.09 cm. The Brooklyn Museum, Brooklyn, New York, Dick S. Ramsay Fund.*

**Tombstones** *by Jacob Lawrence, 1942. Gouache, 28¾" x 20½"/73.02 x 52.07 cm.*
*Collection of the Whitney Museum of American Art, New York.*

**Distillation of Myth** *by Mark Tobey, 1950. Tempera and watercolor, 17" x 23¼"/43.18 x 59.06 cm. Courtesy of Willard Gallery, New York.*

**Wounded Scoter, No. 2** *by Morris Graves, 1944. 18⅞″ x 29⅞″/47.94 x 75.88 cm.*
*The Cleveland Museum of Art, Gift of Gamblers in Modern Art.*

**Vessels of Magic** *by Mark Rothko, c. 1947. 38¾" x 25¾"/98.42 x 65.4 cm. The Brooklyn Museum, Brooklyn, New York.*

**Midnight Quarry** *by William Thon, 1952. 26 ½" x 40"/67.27 x 101.6 cm. Collection of the Whitney Museum of American Art, New York, Wildenstein Benefit Purchase Fund.*

**Black Bush, Autumn, Dogtown** by William Kienbusch, 1954. Casein, 30″ x 40″/76.2 x 101.6 cm. The Roy R. Neuberger Museum, State University of New York, College at Purchase, New York.

# ABOUT THE ARTISTS

**Abbey,** Edwin Austin. Born Philadelphia, Pennsylvania, 1852; died London, England, 1911. Began study of art, 1866; employed by publishing house as draftsman's apprentice and began studying in evening classes, Pennsylvania Academy of the Fine Arts, 1868. Hired as illustrator for Harper & Brothers, New York, 1878. First work exhibited at the American Watercolor Society, 1874. First trip to Europe to gather research for illustrations; visited London, Paris, Munich, and Scotland, 1878 – 81. After brief visit to New York, returned to England, where he settled at Fairford, Gloucestershire, 1882–89. Commissioned to paint mural decoration *Legend of King Arthur* for Boston Public Library, 1890. Elected Associate, Royal Watercolour Society, 1895; Associate, Royal Academy, 1896, and Royal Academician, 1898. Elected Associate, National Academy of Design, New York, 1901; American Academy of Arts and Letters, 1905.

**Anshutz,** Thomas Pollock. Born Newport, Kentucky, 1851; died Fort Washington, Pennsylvania, 1912. Studied at National Academy of Design, New York, 1873 – 75; Pennsylvania Academy of the Fine Arts, 1875 – 81, where he received instruction from Thomas Eakins. Traveled to Paris, enrolled in the Académie des Beaux-Arts and studied under Bouguereau, 1892 – 92. Returned to Philadelphia, resumed teaching at Pennsylvania Academy; instructor in life painting and portraiture until his death in 1912. Elected Associate, National Academy of Design, 1910.

**Audubon,** John James. Born Les Cayes, Haiti, 1785; died New York, New York, 1851. Taken by his father, a French sea captain, to live in Nantes, France, 1791; began drawing birds from nature. Studied briefly with Jacques Louis David before first trip to America, 1803. Returned to France, 1805, continued drawing birds. Emigrated to America, settled near Philadelphia, 1806. Married and moved to Henderson, Kentucky, 1808, where he operated a shop and a mill until 1819. Moved to Cincinnati, Ohio, 1820; taught drawing and worked on his collection of drawings of American birds. Traveled widely thereafter, painting and writing on the birds and mammals of America. Traveled to London, England in search of a publisher for his watercolor drawings, 1826. Lived chiefly in Great Britain until 1839; during this time *Birds of America, Quadrupeds of America,* and *Ornithological Biographies* were all published there. Returned to New York, 1839; began

work on second volume of *Quadrupeds,* published in Philadelphia, 1841. Last expedition to the American West, 1843; traveled up the Missouri River. Two sons, Victor and John Woodhouse, continued their father's work after his death.

**Benson,** Frank Weston. Born Salem, Massachusetts, 1862; died Salem, Massachusetts, 1951. Studied at Boston Museum School of Art, 1880–83; Académie Julian, Paris, under G. Boulanger and J. Lefebvre, 1883 – 85. Returned to United States, 1885; taught at Portland (Maine) Society of Art, 1886 – 87. Opened portrait studio in Boston, 1889; appointed instructor in drawing, Boston Museum School of Art. Began teaching life painting classes at Museum School, 1892. Elected Associate, National Academy of Design, 1897; Academician, 1905. Member "Ten American Painters," organized 1898.

**Benton,** Thomas Hart. Born Neosho, Missouri, 1889; died Kansas City, Missouri, 1975. Studied at Art Institute of Chicago, 1906–07; Académie Julian, Paris, 1908–11. Began professional career as cartoonist, Joplin, Missouri, 1906; turned to painting after his return to the United States from Paris, 1912. Appointed director, department of painting, Kansas City (Missouri) Art Institute, 1935 – 41. Settled in New York, participated in "Forum Exhibition of Modern American Painting," 1916. Employed as draftsman, Norfolk (Virginia) Naval Base, 1918; began to develop interest in themes from American history and folklore. Began series of mural decorations in the Regionalist tradition: New School for Social Research, 1930 – 31; Whitney Museum of American Art, New York, 1932; University of Indiana, Bloomington, 1933; Missouri State Capitol, 1936. Moved from New York, settled permanently in Kansas City, 1935. Elected Associate, National Academy of Design, 1954.

**Birch,** Thomas. Born Warwickshire, England, 1779; died Philadelphia, Pennsylvania, 1851. Brought to America by his father, the engraver William Birch, 1794; settled in Bucks County, Pennsylvania, then moved to Philadelphia, about 1800. Joined in business with his father, published views of Philadelphia under the name "William Birch & Son," 1798–1800. Especially noted for his scenes of naval engagements depicting events of the War of 1812. Traveled extensively in the middle-southern states and New England where he obtained commissions to paint views of private estates and

public buildings. Exhibited regularly at the Pennsylvania Academy of the Fine Arts, and at the National Academy of Design, New York.

**Bishop,** Isabel. Born Cincinnati, Ohio, 1902. Studied at Wicker Art School, Detroit, Michigan, 1917–18; New York School of Applied Design, 1918–20; Art Students League, New York, 1920–22 and 1927–30. Appointed instructor in life painting and composition, Art Students League, New York, 1936 – 37; instructor, Skowhegan (Maine) School of Painting and Sculpture, 1957. Elected Associate, National Academy of Design, 1940; Academician, 1941. Presently maintains a studio in New York.

**Blum,** Robert Frederick. Born Cincinnati, Ohio, 1857; died New York, New York, 1903. Apprenticed as lithographer, 1871; attended night classes at McMicken Art School of Design, Cincinnati. Studied at Pennsylvania Academy of the Fine Arts, 1876; established studio in New York, 1879. Began to achieve success as an illustrator; traveled to Venice, 1890. Visited Japan, on assignment for *Scribner's Magazine,* to illustrate series of articles by Sir Edwin Arnold, 1890 – 93. Thereafter devoted his energies to mural painting—Mendelssohn Hall, New York, his principal work. Elected Academician, National Academy of Design, 1893.

**Bricher,** Alfred Thompson. Born Portsmouth, New Hampshire, 1837; died New Dorp, Staten Island, New York, 1908. Studied art in his leisure time while engaging in business, 1851–58; studied at Lowell Institute, Boston. Became a professional artist, lived and worked in Boston and Newburyport, Massachusetts, 1858 – 68. Moved his studio to New York, 1868. Continued to paint scenes of the Massachusetts and Maine coasts, where he worked during the summer months; known chiefly for his marine paintings. Elected Associate, National Academy of Design, 1879.

**Brown,** George Loring. Born Boston, Massachusetts, 1814; died Malden, Massachusetts, 1889. Apprenticed to a wood engraver; worked as illustrator for a printing company in Lancaster, Massachusetts, 1826–27. First trip to Europe 1831–34; visited Antwerp, London, and Paris. Returned to America; took work as an illustrator in Boston, 1834 – 36. Established a studio in Shrewsbury, Massachusetts and worked briefly in Albany and New York, probably as an itinerant portrait painter, 1836 – 38. Received recognition from prominent Boston artist Washington Allston for work in landscape painting and returned to Europe, 1839. Worked chiefly in Florence and Rome; became known as "Claude" Brown for his landscape paintings in the manner of Claude Lorraine, 1839–59. Returned to America, 1859; worked in New York in 1862 and Boston in 1964. Moved from Boston to Malden, 1879; spent the remainder of his life painting recollections of Italian landscapes, and some scenes in New Hampshire.

**Burchfield,** Charles. Born Ashtabula, Ohio, 1893; died Gardenville, New York, 1967. Studied at Cleveland (Ohio) School of Art under Henry Keller who encouraged him to develop an individual style of painting, 1912–16. Received scholarship to National Academy of Design, New York; returned to Salem, Ohio after only a month in New York, 1916. Inducted into U.S. Army, served in Camouflage Corps, 1918–19. Began to concentrate on painting, traveled to Tennessee and New York, 1920. Moved to Buffalo, New York; designed wallpaper patterns, 1921–29. Rehn Gallery, New York became his dealer; resigned job with wallpaper company to devote full time to painting, 1929. Commissioned by *Fortune* magazine to paint American industrial scenes, 1936–37. Taught painting at various institutions in Buffalo, 1949–52. A prodigious worker, he exhibited in all the major annual watercolor shows until the end of his life.

**Calyo,** Nicolino. Born Naples, Italy, 1799; died New York, New York, 1884. Departed Naples as a political exile, 1821; traveled extensively in Europe, settling for a time in Malta, 1821–29. During this time, he studied art; rejoined his family in Spain. Prompted to leave Spain at outbreak of civil war, sailed for America, 1833. Established studio in Baltimore, Maryland, 1834–35. Moved to New York, 1835; began painting views of the city, later published as wood engravings under the title "Cries of New York." Worked also in Philadelphia, Pennsylvania; Charleston, South Carolina; Richmond, Virginia. Eventually returned to Spain as court painter to Queen Cristina until 1874. Resumed career in New York where he worked until his death.

**Catlin,** George. Born Wilkes-Barre, Pennsylvania, 1796; died Jersey City, New Jersey, 1872. Studied law, Litchfield, Connecticut, 1817–18. Began teaching himself painting while reading law; moved to Philadelphia and set up studio as miniature portrait painter, 1820–25. Became itinerant portrait painter in New York State, 1825–29. Moved to Richmond, Virginia as portrait painter, 1829. Resolved to create an "Indian Gallery" of portraits; first trip up the Missouri River to Fort Union, 1832. Periodically continued to visit Far West, painting Indian portraits and scenes of tri-

bal life, 1833–36. Opened his "Indian Gallery" in New York, exhibited 494 paintings of Plains, Woodlands, and South Eastern Indians, 1837. Traveled with his collection of paintings to England and the Continent, 1839–52. Returned about that time to America, visiting Idaho and South America. Final trip to Europe lasted from 1858–70; returned to New York.

**Champney,** James Wells. Born Boston, Massachusetts, 1843; died New York, New York, 1903. Studied drawing at Lowell (Massachusetts) Institute; worked as wood engraver until 1860. Enlisted in 45th Massachusetts Volunteers; served at Gettysburg and in South Carolina, 1860–64. After the war, taught drawing in Lexington, Massachusetts. Sailed for Europe; studied under Edouard Frere at Écouen, France, 1866. Studied at the Royal Academy, Antwerp, Belgium, 1868. Lived in Paris for a year and returned to Boston in 1870. Commissioned by *Scribner's Monthly* to illustrate life in the South, 1873; became recognized internationally for his work. Appointed Professor of Art, Smith College, Northampton, Massachusetts, 1877; continued to illustrate for Scribner's. Frequent trips to Europe, 1880–90; came to regard Paris as his second home. Elected Associate, National Academy of Design, 1882.

**Chase,** William Merritt. Born Franklin, Indiana, 1849; died New York, New York, 1916. Studied portrait painting under Benjamin Hayes in Indianapolis, 1867–69. Studied at National Academy of Design, New York, under L. E. Wilmarth, 1869–70. Enrolled in Royal Academy, Munich, Germany, 1872; studied under Alexander Wagner and Karl von Piloty. Came under the influence of Wilhelm Leibl and his group of realist painters; shared studio with Frank Duveneck, 1875. Awarded medal for painting, Centennial Exposition, Philadelphia, 1876. Returned to New York; began teaching at Art Students League, 1878. Trips to Spain and Holland, 1881–85. Elected Associate, National Academy of Design, 1889. Began teaching at Brooklyn Museum School of Art, 1890, and at summer art school at Shinnecock, Long Island, 1891. Founded "The Chase School" in New York, 1896; continued teaching there until 1908. Joined "Ten American Painters" group, 1902. Elected Academician, National Academy of Design, 1890.

**Coleman,** Samuel. Born Portland, Maine, 1832 or 1833; died New York, New York, 1920. Received his early education in New York, where he also studied painting under Asher B. Durand. First painting exhibited at the National Academy of Design, 1851; paintings included in annual shows thereafter. Elected Associate, National Academy of Design, 1855; Academician, 1862. Founder and first president, American Soc-

iety of Painters in Water Colors, 1866. Made two trips to Europe, 1860–62 and 1871–75; traveled extensively in Northern Europe and the Mediterranean. Traveled to the Far West and California between 1868 and 1871. Known as a connoisseur of Oriental art as well as an ardent supporter of American artists.

**Cropsey,** Jasper Francis. Born Rossville, Staten Island, New York, 1823; died, Hastings-on-Hudson, New York, 1900. Worked as an architect's apprentice, New York, 1837–41. Began to study painting; worked from nature on trips to New Jersey, Connecticut, and the Hudson River Valley, 1844–46. Traveled to Europe, settled for a time in Rome, 1847–49. Returned to the United States; periodic sketching trips throughout New England, New York, and Pennsylvania, 1849–56. Sold all of his paintings for a trip to England; remained there for seven years, 1856–63. Elected Academician, National Academy of Deisgn, 1851. Established his residence and studio at Hastings-on-Hudson, 1864; became known for his autumnal landscape paintings. Continued his interest in architecture; designed a number of private residences in the 1870s and 1880s. Widely recognized as a major artist: held memberships in every important art society in the United States.

**Davies,** Arthur Bowen. Born Utica, New York, 1862; died Florence, Italy, 1928. Studied at the Art Institute of Chicago while employed as draftsman for Chicago Board of Trade, 1878–79. Worked in Mexico as a civil engineer draftsman, 1880–82; became interested in Spanish Colonial religious painting. Moved to New York, supported himself as an illustrator for *St. Nicholas* magazine while attending classes at the Art Students League, 1886–88. First painting exhibited at American Art Association Galleries, New York, 1888; began devoting full time to painting. First trip to Europe sponsored by Benjamin Altman, the collector, 1893. First one-man exhibition, Macbeth Gallery, New York, 1894. Organized the "Eight American Painters" exhibition, New York, 1908; was formative influence in organizing the International Exhibition of Modern Art (the Armory Show), New York, 1913. Began experiments in other media, including lithography and watercolor; incorporated stylistic elements of modernism with theories about classical art, 1920–28.

**Davis,** Joseph. Birth and death dates unknown, active 1832–37. An itinerant folk artist, known only for watercolor portraits. Worked principally in Maine and New Hampshire. Over one hundred works are attributed to him from stylistic evidence in three signed examples. Sometimes referred to as the "Left Hand Painter" because of his habit of facing his subjects to the right.

**Davis,** Stuart. Born Philadelphia, Pennsylvania; 1894; died New York, New York, 1969. Left high school to study with Robert Henri in New York; painting accepted in the Exhibition of Independent Artists, New York, 1910. Commissioned as illustrator for *The Masses* and *Harper's Weekly;* exhibited five watercolors in the Armory Show, New York, 1913. Began summer painting trips to Gloucester, Massachusetts, 1915; returned almost yearly until 1934. First one-man exhibition, Sheridan Square Gallery, New York, 1917. Service with U.S. Army Intelligence Department, as mapmaker, 1918. Worked in Paris, 1928 – 29. Began teaching at Art Students League, New York, 1931. Participated in Museum of Modern Art mural exhibition, New York, 1932; commissioned to paint mural for Radio City Music Hall, New York. Enrolled in Federal Art Project, 1933. Elected national chairman, Artists Congress, 1938. Retrospective exhibition, Museum of Modern Art, New York, 1945.

**Deas,** Charles. Born Philadelphia, Pennsylvania, 1818; died St. Louis, Missouri, 1867. After failing to be appointed as cadet to West Point, decided to become an artist, 1836. Studied painting in New York; exhibited first painting at National Academy of Design, 1838; elected to membership in the Academy, 1839. Trip to Ft. Crawford, Wisconsin, 1840; remained in the West for seven years, principally in St. Louis. Submitted paintings to annual exhibitions of the National Academy, 1847 – 49. Gradually afflicted with mental illness; died in an asylum.

**Demuth,** Charles. Born Lancaster, Pennsylvania, 1883; died Lancaster, Pennsylvania, 1935. Studied art at Drexel Institute, Philadelphia, Pennsylvania, 1901; Pennsylvania Academy of the Fine Arts, under Thomas Anshutz and William Merritt Chase, 1905. Worked independently in Paris, 1907; returned to the Pennsylvania Academy. Studied in Paris at various art academies: Moderne, Colarossi, and Julian, 1912 – 14. Began to exhibit regularly at Daniel Gallery, New York, 1915 – 25. After 1915 worked mainly in Lancaster, also maintaining a studio in New York during winters of 1914 and 1915. Summer painting trips to Provincetown, Massachusetts, 1914 – 21. Frequently ill during last fifteen years of his life, but continued to work actively until his death.

**Dickinson,** Preston. Born New York, New York, 1891; died Catalonia, Spain, 1930. Studied under Ernest Lawson at Art Students League, New York, before 1910. Independent study in Paris, worked from Old Master paintings in the Louvre, 1910 – 15. Exhibited in *Salon des Artistes Français,* 1912. First one-man show at Daniel Gallery, New York, 1924. Joined Whitney Studio Club,

New York, 1925. Frequent trips to Canada; one-man exhibition, Quebec, 1926 – 27. Returned to Europe to secure a studio; died suddenly while traveling, 1930.

**Dove,** Arthur. Born Canandaigua, New York, 1880; died Huntington, Long Island, New York, 1946. Graduated Cornell University, Ithaca, New York, 1903. Worked as free-lance illustrator, New York City, for *Collier's, McCalls, Saturday Evening Post,* 1904 – 06. First trip to Europe, painted in southern France, 1907 – 08. Resumed work as illustrator, New York, 1909. Exhibited at Stieglitz's "291" Gallery, New York, 1910. Began lifelong friendship with collector Duncan Phillips, Washington, D.C., 1926; work included in first American museum exhibition at The Brooklyn Museum. Invited to exhibit in Whitney Museum of American Art, New York, First Biennial, 1932. First one-man show of watercolors, Springfield (Massachusetts) Museum of Fine Arts, 1933. Included in *Ten American Watercolor Painters* exhibition, Museum of Fine Arts, Boston, 1939. In spite of severe illness, continued to work actively until his death.

**Durand,** Asher Brown. Born Jefferson Village, New Jersey, 1796; died Jefferson Village, New Jersey, 1886. Apprenticed to engraver Peter Maverick, Newark, New Jersey, 1812–17. Published his engraving after painting by John Trumbull, *Declaration of Independence,* 1823. Became one of the original fifteen founders of the National Academy of Design, New York, 1826. Received first commission from collector Luman Reed, 1834. Ceased work as an engraver to devote himself to painting; commissioned by Reed to paint a set of presidential portraits, 1835. Turned to landscape painting, influenced by Thomas Cole, 1837 – 39. Traveled to Europe, visited England and the Continent, 1840 – 41. Elected president, National Academy of Design, 1845.

**Eakins,** Thomas. Born Philadelphia, Pennsylvania, 1844; died Philadelphia, Pennsylvania, 1916. Studied drawing at The Pennsylvania Academy of the Fine Arts; anatomy at Jefferson Medical College, Philadelphia, 1861–66. Traveled to Paris, enrolled in the École des Beaux-Arts, studied under J. L. Gérôme, 1866–68. Trip to Spain, studied Velásquez and Murillo, 1869. Exhibited *The Gross Clinic* at Centennial Exposition, Philadelphia; began teaching classes in anatomy, Pennsylvania Academy of the Fine Arts, 1876. Appointed professor of anatomy, Pennsylvania Academy, 1879. Joined Society of American Artists, 1880. Began work in photography, recording human and animal locomotion, 1884. Appointed director, Pennsylvania Academy, 1882; tenure lasted until 1886 when forced to resign. Began teaching at Art Students

League of Philadelphia. Summer painting trip to the Dakotas, 1887. Taught at National Academy of Design, New York, 1888–94; elected Academician, 1902. After years of neglect, Pennsylvania Academy awarded him its highest honor for painting, 1904.

**Eastman,** Seth. Born Brunswick, Maine, 1808; died Washington, D.C., 1875. Appointed to West Point, 1824; graduated 1829. Assigned to Ft. Crawford, Wisconsin, 1829; Ft. Snelling, Minnesota, 1831. Sketched Indian life and made topographical drawings. Instructor in drawing, West Point, New York, 1833–40. Assigned to Bureau of Indian Affairs, Washington, D.C. to make illustrations for official publication on Indian life, 1850–55. Commissioned by Congress to paint documentary series on western military subjects, 1867.

**Farny,** Henry François. Born Ribeauville, Alsace, France, 1847; died Cincinnati, Ohio, 1916. Emigrated with family to the United States, 1853; lived near Warren, Pennsylvania. Family settled in Cincinnati, Ohio, 1859. Traveled to Europe; studied in Rome, Düsseldorf, Vienna, and Munich, 1866–70. Second trip to Europe; associated with Frank Duveneck in Munich, 1873. Commissioned to illustrate for *McGuffey Readers,* 1879. Trip to Dakota Territory, began study of Indian life, 1881. Sketching trip down Missouri River from Helena to the Great Falls, 1884; illustrations published in *The Century Magazine,* 1888. Trip to Ft. Sill, Oklahoma to sketch Apache Indians. Worked in Cincinnati for the remainder of his life; turned from illustration to painting.

**Feininger,** Lyonel. Born New York, New York, 1871; died New York, New York, 1956. Studied violin with his father in New York, 1880–83. Visited Germany to study music; decided to become painter, 1887. Studied in Berlin and Hamburg, 1887–91; in Paris at Académie Colarossi, 1892. Returned to Berlin, became illustrator, 1893–1906. Exhibited with "The Blue Rider" group of painters, Berlin, 1913. Taught painting and graphic arts at Bauhaus, Weimar, 1919–24. Appointed Artist in Residence at Bauhaus, Dessau. Became founding member of "The Blue Four," 1924. Taught summer sessions at Mills College, Oakland, California, 1936–37; took up permanent residence in New York, 1937.

**Glackens,** William James. Born Philadelphia, Pennsylvania, 1870; died Westport, Connecticut, 1938. Worked as artist-reporter for Philadelphia press, 1891; colleagues included John Sloan, George B. Luks, and Everett Shinn. Attended night classes, Pennsylvania Academy of the Fine Arts, Philadelphia; studied under Thomas Anshutz, 1892. Trip to Holland and France with Robert Henri, 1895. Returned to New

York; began exhibiting paintings, 1896. Exhibited in the "Eight American Painters" show, Macbeth Gallery, New York, 1908. Helped organize the exhibition of the "Independents," 1910. Chairman for committee of selection, American section, the Armory Show, New York, 1913. Elected first president, Society of Independent Artists, 1917. Made annual painting trips to France, 1925–32. Elected Academician, National Academy of Design, 1933.

**Graves,** Morris Cole. Born Fox Valley, Oregon, 1910. Mainly self-taught as a painter; traveled in Japan and China, 1928–30. First recognition for his work at Seattle Art Museum, awarded prize for painting, 1933; one-man show, Seattle Art Museum, 1936. Joined WPA Federal Art Project, 1936–39. Traveled in Europe, 1938–39. Briefly studied with Mark Tobey; around 1937 began to work in watercolor techniques relating to study of Oriental art. Awarded Guggenheim fellowship, 1946. First one-man show abroad, Oslo, Norway, 1955; in the United States, Whitney Museum of American Art, New York, 1956. Elected member, National Institute of Arts and Letters, New York, 1956. Presently lives in Loleta, California.

**Grosz,** George. Born Berlin, Germany, 1893; died Berlin, Germany, 1959. Studied at Royal Saxon Academy of the Fine Arts, Dresden, 1910; Royal Arts and Crafts School, Berlin, 1911. Traveled to Paris, enrolled in Académie Colarossi, 1913. Active as illustrator for Berlin periodicals, 1913 and 1919. First one-man show, Berlin, 1918. Active as theatrical designer, 1920–30. First one-man show of watercolors in the United States, Weyhe Gallery, New York, 1931. Taught at Art Students League, New York, 1932. Emigrated with family from Germany, settled in New York, 1933; resumed teaching at Art Students League until 1936. Granted United States citizenship, 1938. Taught at School of Fine Arts, Columbia University, New York, 1941–42.

**Hamilton,** James. Born Entrien, Ireland, 1819; died San Francisco, California, 1878. Emigrated with family to Philadelphia, 1834. Largely self-taught, but was active as a drawing instructor; pupils included Thomas and Edward Moran. Exhibited for the first time at Gallery of the Artists' Fund Society, Philadelphia, 1840; Pennsylvania Academy of the Fine Arts, 1843. Exhibited at National Academy of Design, New York, 1846. Made illustrations for *The Pictorial History of the American Navy*, 1845; illustrated Dr. Elisha Kane's *Arctic Explorations*, published 1856–57. Traveled to England, 1854; was greatly influenced by works of Turner. Painting trip to New England, 1869; visited Boston, Cape Cod, and Newport. In Philadelphia, 1875, sold large collection of his own paintings to raise funds for a world tour. Arrived in San Francisco, 1876, where he worked until his death.

**Hart,** George Overbury "Pop." Born Cairo, Illinois, 1868; died Coytesville, New York, 1933. Worked as newspaper illustrator, Chicago; studied at Art Institute of Chicago, before 1900. Trip to Italy and Egypt, 1900; to Mexico, Central America, San Francisco, 1900–03. Visited Tahiti, Samoa, Hawaii, 1903–04. Traveled in northern Europe, 1905–07; studied art in Paris, 1907. Worked as sign painter in New York and New Jersey, 1907–12; movie set painter in Fort Lee, New Jersey, 1912–20. Extensive travel in the West Indies, 1916–22; Mexico, 1923–29. Trip to Morocco, Spain, and France, 1929–30. Failing health confined him in last years to his studio in Coytesville, New York.

**Harvey,** George. Born Tottenham, England, c. 1800; died London (?), England, 1878. Arrived in New York, 1820; traveled in the West, gathering sketches until about 1822. Began career as miniature portrait painter in New York, 1827. Elected Associate, National Academy of Design, New York, 1828. Moved to Boston, 1829. Returned to London for further training; exhibited at the Royal Academy, 1832. Lived in Boston as portrait painter, 1833–35; moved to Hastings-on-Hudson, New York and began working on watercolors intended for publication as *Scenes of the Primitive Forest of America at the Four Periods of the Year*, 1841. Between 1848 and 1857, made frequent trips to England. Maintained studio in New York, 1871–72.

**Haseltine,** William Stanley. Born Philadelphia, Pennsylvania, 1835; died Rome, Italy, 1900. Studied painting with Paul Weber in Philadelphia, 1850. Graduated from Harvard, 1854; went to Düsseldorf, Germany to study art, 1855. Became pupil of Andreas Achenbach, a landscape painter. Sketching trip of the Rhine Valley in company of Albert Bierstadt, Emanuel Leutze, and Worthington Whittredge, 1856; trip to Rome 1857. Returned to America, 1858; established studio in New York. Moved permanently to Rome, 1869; occasional summer trip to the United States and sketching tours of the Continent thereafter. Appointed to committee to select works by American artists living in Italy for World's Columbian Exposition, Chicago, 1893. Painting trip to Maine, 1895; West Coast and Alaska, 1895. Elected Academician, National Academy of Design, New York, 1861.

**Hassam,** Frederick Childe. Born Dorchester, Massachusetts, 1859; died East Hampton, Long Island, New York, 1935. Employed in Boston as an illustrator, 1878. Trip to Britain, Netherlands, Spain, and Italy, 1883. Second European trip, 1886–89; settled in Paris and came under influence of Impressionism. Exhibited in Salon of 1888 and Paris Exposition of 1889. Returned to New York, 1889; began summer painting trip to New England. Trip to Havana, Cuba, 1895. Trip to France and Italy, 1897. Joined "Ten American Painters" group, 1898. Taught at Art Students League, New York, 1898–99. Painting trips to Oregon, 1908; Paris, 1910. Elected Academician, National Academy of Design, New York, 1906. Exhibited in the Armory Show, New York, 1913. Established summer studio at East Hampton, Long Island, New York, 1920.

**Heade,** Martin Johnson. Born Lumberville, Pennsylvania, 1819; died St. Augustine, Florida, 1904. Before 1837, studied briefly with Edward Hicks, primitive Pennsylvania painter. Trip to Europe, 1837–40; visited Italy, France, and England. Established a studio in New York, 1843; Philadelphia, 1847; St. Louis, 1852. Worked in Chicago, speculated in real estate, 1853–56. Established a studio in New York, 1859. Extensive travel, 1861–66; painting trips to New England, Brazil, and London. Maintained studio in New York, 1866–81, while continuing to travel frequently. Final trip to South America, 1870. Moved his studio to Washington, D.C., 1881; to St. Augustine in 1885.

**Henry,** Edward Lamson. Born Charleston, South Carolina, 1841; died Ellenville, New York, 1919. Studied at Pennsylvania Academy of the Fine Arts, Philadelphia, 1858. Lived in Paris, 1860–62; was a student of Gleyre. Returned to New York, established a career as a painter, 1862–64. Brief military service, U. S. Army, 1864; painted his first Civil War subject, 1865. Elected Associate, National Academy of Design, New York, 1867; Academician, 1869. Settled at Cragsmoor, New York, 1884; began to paint scenes of New York State country life. Exhibited at World's Columbian Exposition, Chicago, 1893.

**Hill,** John Henry. Born West Nyack, New York, 1839; died West Nyack, New York, 1922. Son of John William Hill, of the family of English engravers who emigrated to America in 1816; was taught drawing and engraving by his father. Frequent sketching tours of New England and New York State; trip to White Mountains, New Hampshire, 1857. Elected Associate for one year, National Academy of Design, 1858–59. Trip to London, 1864–65; studied works of Turner. Published folio of 24 etchings, *Sketches from Nature*, about 1867. Accompanied the King surveying expedition to Far West, 1868. Greatly influenced by John Ruskin's theories of art; returned to England and the Continent on a painting tour, 1879. Published *An Artist's Memorial* in honor of his father, 1888; illustrated with etchings from the paintings of J. W. Hill.

**Hill,** John William. Born London (?), England, 1812; died West Nyack, New York, 1879. Son of John Hill (1770–1850), the engraver of William Guy Wall's paintings for *Hudson River Portfolio* (1820–25). Emigrated to Philadelphia, 1819. Family moved to New York, 1822; apprenticed to his father, learned drawing, engraving, and watercolor painting. Began making watercolor views of the Hudson River Valley and environs. Family moved to West Nyack, New York, 1836; J. W. Hill became topographical artist for New York State Geological Survey. Later employed by Smith Brothers, New York, to make views of American cities. Work greatly influenced by John Ruskin's *Modern Painters*, about 1855. Elected Associate, National Academy of Design, 1833. Exhibited with American Society of Painters in Watercolors, 1867.

**Hirst,** Claude Raguet. Born New York, New York (?), 1855; died New York, New York, 1942. Details of her life and career are extremely few. Exhibited four paintings, National Academy of Design, New York, 1884; three paintings in the exhibition of 1885. Studio on East 14th Street, New York, adjacent to that of William M. Harnett, 1886; began to change subject matter from flowers and fruit to books on tabletop. Exhibited such subjects in annual exhibition of National Academy, 1891 and 1896. She married William C. Fitler, who died, New York, 1911. Hirst died in obscurity and extreme poverty.

**Homer,** Winslow. Born Boston, Massachusetts, 1836; died Prout's Neck, Maine, 1910. Apprenticed to J. H. Bufford, lithographer, Boston, about 1854. Began career as free-lance illustrator, 1857; worked for *Harper's Weekly.* Moved to New York City, 1859; studied at National Academy of Design night school, about 1861. First lessons in oil painting under Frederick Rondel, 1861. Made trips to war zones, sketched life in the Union Army for *Harper's*, 1861–62; occasional trips to the front, 1863–65. Elected Associate, National Academy of Design, 1864; Academician, 1865. Trip to France, worked in Paris and Picardy, 1867. First watercolors, Gloucester, Massachusetts, 1873; further development of watercolor style, Mountainville, New York, summer 1878. Lived in Tynemouth, England, 1881–82. Settled at Prout's Neck, Maine, 1883. Winter trip to Nassau, Bahamas, 1884–85; Santiago de Cuba, 1885. Winter trips to Florida for watercolor painting, 1886 and 1890; Adirondack watercolors, summers of 1889 and 1891–92. Watercolor painting in Quebec, summers of 1895 and 1897. Trips to Nassau, Bahamas, and Bermuda, 1898–99; Florida, 1903–04. Last watercolor, *Diamond Shoal*, 1905. Became ill the summer of 1906; suffered paralytic stroke, 1908. Few works completed from that time until his death.

**Hopper,** Edward. Born Nyack, New York, 1882; died New York, New York, 1967. Studied at New York School of Art, under Robert Henri, 1900–06. First trip to Paris, 1906; brief return visits, 1909 and 1910. Exhibited in the Armory Show, New York, 1913, and sold his first picture. Turned to commercial illustration for livelihood, 1915–25; began work in etching. First one-man show, Whitney Studio Club, New York, 1920. Began painting in watercolor; first museum purchase, The Brooklyn Museum, 1923. Exhibited watercolors at Rehn Gallery, New York, 1924, and sold entire group. Trip to New Mexico, 1925. Second one-man show at Rehn Gallery, 1927; retrospective exhibition, Museum of Modern Art, New York, 1933. Built summer studio at Truro, Cape Cod, Massachusetts, 1930; began concentrating on New England subjects. Retrospective exhibitions, Whitney Museum of American Art, New York, 1950 and 1964. Elected to National Institute of Arts and Letters, 1945; American Academy of Arts and Letters, 1955.

**Inness,** George. Born Newburgh, New York, 1825; died Bridge of Allan, Scotland, 1894. Studied briefly under Régis Ginoux in Brooklyn, 1846; largely self-taught. Work included in first exhibition, American Society of Painters in Watercolors, New York, 1866. Sent to Europe for study by patron, 1850; settled in Italy and was influenced by works of Claude and Poussin. Stayed briefly in Paris, 1854; elected Associate, National Academy of Design, New York. Settled in Medfield, Massachusetts, 1859. Moved to Perth Amboy, New Jersey, 1864. Represented in American art section, Paris Exposition of 1867. Elected Academician, National Academy of Design, 1868. Trip to Europe, 1870–74; painted in Rome, Paris, and Barbizon. Worked in Boston and New York, 1875–78. Settled permanently in Montclair, New Jersey, 1878. Painting trips to Virginia, 1884, and Yosemite, California, 1891.

**Johnston,** David Claypoole. Born Philadelphia, Pennsylvania, 1799; died Dorchester, Massachusetts, 1865. Apprenticed to the engraver Francis Kearney, Philadelphia, 1815–19. Established his own business, produced prints dealing with social caricature. Briefly turned to acting, 1821–25, in Philadelphia and Boston. Exhibited paintings at the Boston Athenaeum, 1829–61. Resumed career as social caricaturist in Boston; issued annual series of comic plates, *Scraps*, 1830–49.

**Keith,** William. Born Old Meldrum, Aberdeenshire, Scotland, 1838 or 1839; died Berkeley, California, 1911. Emigrated to United States with his family, 1851. Apprenticed to a wood engraver; worked for *Harper's Weekly* until 1859. Settled in San Francisco, California; worked as commercial wood engraver, 1859. Sketching trip to Oregon, 1868. Studied in Düsseldorf under Albert Flamm, 1870. Returned to United States, painted landscapes in Maine, 1871. Established studio in Boston, shared with William Hahn, 1872. Returned to California, 1872. Several trips to Europe: 1883, 1893, and 1899; the latter to Amsterdam where he studied works of Rembrandt.

**Kienbusch,** William Austin. Born New York, New York, 1914. Studied art history, Princeton University, graduated magna cum laude, 1936. Studied with Henry Varnum Poor, Stuart Davis, and Anton Refregier in New York until 1942. Studied at Art Students League, New York, 1936–37. Began summer visits to Maine, 1946; influenced by works of Marsden Hartley and John Marin. First one-man show, Kraushaar Galleries, New York, 1949. Represented in exhibition *New Decade*, Whitney Museum of American Art, New York, 1955. Awarded Guggenheim Fellowship; painted in Crete, 1958. Taught at Brooklyn Museum School of Art, 1948–69. Presently maintains winter studio in New York; summer, Cranberry Isle, Maine.

**Kingman,** Dong. Born Oakland, California, 1911. Studied traditional Chinese painting, Hong Kong, 1924–26. Awarded Guggenheim Fellowships, 1942 and 1943. Appointed instructor in art, Columbia University, New York, 1946–54; instructor in watercolor and history of Chinese art, Hunter College, New York, 1948–53. Sponsored by U. S. Department of State, world lecture tour, 1954. Worked as mural painter since 1942; book illustrator since 1946. Works presently in New York.

**Krimmel,** John Lewis. Born Württemberg, Germany, 1787; died Germantown, Pennsylvania, 1821. Emigrated to United States, 1810; in Philadelphia, joined a brother in business. Immediately began painting portraits and genre scenes of Philadelphia; exhibited at Pennsylvania Academy of the Fine Arts, 1811. Trip to Germany, 1817–19; returned to Philadelphia. Genre paintings engraved and published by Alexander Lawson, Philadelphia. Elected president, Society of American Artists, 1821.

**La Farge,** John. Born New York, New York, 1835; died Providence, Rhode Island, 1910. Received early instruction in drawing from his grandfather, Binsse de St. Victor; studied law and architecture. Studied briefly under Thomas Couture in Paris, 1856; traveled to Munich and London. Became influenced by English Pre-Raphaelite painters. Returned to United States; studied with William Morris Hunt in Newport, Rhode Island, 1859. Worked as landscape painter; became interested in techniques of stained-glass design. Second trip to Europe, 1873. Commissioned to execute first large-scale mural decoration in America, Trinity Church, Boston, 1876; became president, Society of Mural Painters. Numerous commissions for church windows, New York, in 1877–90. Trip to Japan, 1886; Tahiti and Samoa, 1890–91; France, 1899. Accompanied by the writer Henry Adams on all travels. Elected Academician, National Academy of Design, New York, 1869.

**Latrobe,** Benjamin. Born Fulneck, Yorkshire, England, 1764; died New Orleans, Louisiana, 1820. Worked in London as an architect until 1795; emigrated to Norfolk, Virginia. Designed Bank of Pennsylvania, Philadelphia, 1798. Selected by Thomas Jefferson to complete the Capitol, Washington, D.C., 1803; later to renovate the interior, 1815–17. Designed Baltimore (Maryland) Cathedral, built between 1804 and 1821, considered his most important project. Also designed domestic architecture; Commodore Decatur house, Washington, D.C., 1817–18, a notable example.

**Lawrence,** Jacob. Born Atlantic City, New Jersey, 1917. Studied with Charles Alston in New York, 1932–39; associated with Harlem Workshop. Worked in WPA Federal Art Project, 1934–38. Began first series of paintings dealing with black history, 1936. Awarded scholarship to American Artists School, 1937; studied under Anton Refregier. First one-man show, Downtown Gallery, New York, 1941. First major thematic series, group of sixty tempera paintings, *The Migration of the Negro,* 1940–41. Taught at Black Mountain College at invitation of Josef Albers, 1946. Awarded Guggenheim Fellowship, 1946. Appointed instructor in painting, Pratt Institute, Brooklyn, 1956–71; Professor of Art, University of Washington, Seattle, 1970 to present.

**Leutze,** Emanuel Gottlieb. Born Gmünd, Bavaria, 1816; died Washington, D.C., 1868. Brought to America as a child by his parents; settled in Philadelphia. Studied painting with John Rubens Smith in Philadelphia; painted portraits in Churchtown, Pennsylvania, 1836. Patron Edward L. Carey sent him to study in Düsseldorf, 1841; was pupil of Karl Friedrick Lessing. Traveled to Munich and Rome; established his studio in Düsseldorf, 1845. Painted *Washington Crossing the Delaware,* 1851. Frequently submitted historical paintings to exhibitions of National Academy of Design; elected Academician, National Academy, 1860. Represented in first exhibition of American Society of Painters in Water Colors, 1867. Returned to United States permanently, 1959; Congress commissioned him to paint mural for House of Representatives, 1861.

**Luks,** George Benjamin. Born Williamsport, Pennsylvania, 1867; died New York, New York, 1933. Studied at Pennsylvania Academy of the Fine Arts until about 1885. Trip to Europe, studied at Düsseldorf Academy; independent work in Europe until 1894. Returned to United States, joined Philadelphia *Press* as illustrator, 1894. Formed friendships with artists associated with Robert Henri. Sent to Cuba as illustrator for Philadelphia *Evening Bulletin,* 1895; employed as illustrator for New York *World,* 1896. Encouraged by William Glackens to paint, 1897; exhibited at National Arts Club, New York, 1904. Participated in "The Eight" exhibition, Macbeth Gallery, New York, 1908. Exhibited in the Armory Show, New York, 1913. Awarded Hudnut Prize, New York Water Color Club, 1916. Painting trips to Maine, 1922; Nova Scotia, 1927. Taught at Art Students League New York before forming his own school.

**MacKnight,** Dodge. Born Providence, Rhode Island, 1860; died East Sandwich, Massachusetts, 1950. Studied at Atelier Cormon, Paris, about 1886. Associated with Vincent Van Gogh, who urged him to join artists' brotherhood at Arles, along with Gauguin. Trip to Arles, North Africa, and Spain; returned to United States, 1888. Remained in New England for the rest of his life, with brief trips to Mexico and the Mediterranean. Found critical acceptance for his work in Boston largely through the patronage of Isabella Stewart Gardner.

**Marin,** John. Born Rutherford, New Jersey, 1870; died Cape Split, Maine, 1953. Began painting in watercolor, 1888. Trained as architect, Stevens Institute, New York; opened his own office, 1893. Studied painting at Pennsylvania Academy of the Fine Arts, 1899–1901; pupil of Thomas Anshutz and Hugh Breckenridge. Studied at Art Students League, New York, 1904; pupil of Frank Dumond. Trip to Europe 1905; settled in Paris with summer trips to Holland, Italy, and England, until 1910. Met Alfred Steiglitz in Paris, 1909; invited to exhibit watercolors at Steiglitz' Gallery "291," New York. First one-man show, New York, 1910; trip to Tyrol in the spring. Returned to United States permanently, 1911. Summer painting trips to the Berkshire Hills, Massachusetts, 1911–12. Established winter studio at Cliffside, New Jersey, 1916. First summer painting trip to Maine, 1914; summer residence at Stonington, Maine, 1919–24. Trip to Taos and Santa Fe, New Mexico, 1929–30. Permanent summer studio at Cape Split, Maine, 1933–53. Retrospective exhibitions included Museum of Modern Art, New York, 1936; Institute of Contemporary Art, Boston, 1947; M. H. de Young Museum, San Francisco, 1949; Venice Biennale, Italy, 1950; American Academy of Arts and Letters, New York,

1954. Elected member, American Institute of Arts and Letters, 1945.

**Marsh,** Reginald. Born Paris, France, 1898; died Dorset, Vermont, 1954. Came with parents to United States, 1900; settled in Nutley, New Jersey. Entered Yale University, 1916; contributed drawings to Yale *Record* and became its art editor. Received first professional art instruction at Yale, and at Art Students League, New York, 1919. Graduated Yale University, 1920; moved to New York and worked as illustrator for *Evening Post, Herald, Vanity Fair,* and *Harper's Bazaar.* Staff artist for New York *Daily News,* 1922–25; illustrator for *New Yorker,* 1925–31. Studied painting at Art Students League, New York, 1920–24; pupil of John Sloan, Kenneth H. Miller, and George Luks. First one-man show, Whitney Studio Club, New York, 1924. First trip to Europe, 1925–26; worked principally in Paris. Established a permanent studio on Union Square, New York, 1937. Began monumental watercolors, produced more than forty, 1939–40. War correspondent for *Life* in South America, 1943. Painting trip to the West Indies, 1950. Elected Associate, National Academy of Design, 1937; Academician, 1943.

**Martin,** Homer Dodge. Born Albany, New York, 1836; died St. Paul Minnesota, 1897. Studied landscape painting under James M. Hart, National Academy of Design, New York, 1862. Moved to Tenth Street Studio Building, New York; associates included Sanford R. Gifford, Eastman Johnson, and John La Farge. Summer painting trips to the Adirondack Mountains, New York, 1864–69. Elected Associate, National Academy of Design, 1869; Academician, 1875. Trip to France and England, 1876; influenced by James Whistler. Founder, Society of American Artists, 1878. Trip to England and Normandy, France, 1881–82. Commissioned by *Century Magazine* to illustrate views of England, 1885. Returned to New York, 1887; eyesight progressively deteriorated. Last years spent in St. Paul, 1892–97.

**McCloskey,** William John. Active 1879–91. Almost no biographical information is available on this artist; aside from exhibition records, there is no indication of where he might have established his studios. Studied at the Pennsylvania Academy of the Fine Arts; exhibited in student show, 1879. Probably a pupil of Thomas Eakins. Listed in Philadelphia directories, 1880–85; New York in 1889. Exhibited at the National Academy of Design, New York, 1888–91; the Brooklyn Art Association, 1891. Small still life paintings in oil and watercolor constitute his only known work.

**Middleton,** John Izard. Born near Charleston, South Carolina, 1785; died Paris, France, 1849. The family house, Middleton

Place, near Charleston was the gathering place for persons of literary, musical, and artistic accomplishment. Educated in England, he spent the greater part of his adult life in France and Italy. Was considered the first American classical archeologist; made his own watercolor renderings for engraved illustrations in his principal scholarly work, *Grecian Remains in Italy*, published in 1812. Moved permanently to Paris about 1819; became a prominent collector of paintings.

**Miller,** Alfred Jacob. Born Baltimore, Maryland, 1810; died Baltimore, Maryland, 1874. Studied portrait painting under Thomas Sully in Philadelphia, 1831–32; studied at École des Beaux-Arts, Paris, 1833. Trips to Rome, Florence, and Venice; returned to Baltimore, 1834, and established a studio there until 1837. Trip to New Orleans, Louisiana; joined expedition of William Drummond Stewart to Wyoming Territory, summer, 1837. Returned to Baltimore, 1838; worked from sketches made in Wyoming. Exhibited works at Apollo Gallery, New York; traveled to Scotland, 1840. Returned to Baltimore, 1842; spent the rest of his life as successful portrait painter in that city.

**Miller,** William Ricarby. Born near Darlington, England, 1818; died West Chester, New York, 1893. Received early lessons in drawing from father, Joseph Miller; began to work steadily as landscape painter in Durham and Northumberland, about 1836. Emigrated to America in 1844 or 1845; settled in New York where he remained for the rest of his life. Contributed works in watercolor to the American Art-Union, New York, 1848. During the following decade, made illustrations for *Gleason's Pictorial, Leslie's Illustrated Weekly Newspaper,* and *Ballou's Pictorial.* Frequent exhibitor at the National Academy of Design, New York, 1853–76. Began his most ambitious project, *1000 Gems,* picturesque landscape views of England and America, about 1873; project remained unfinished at his death, and was never published as intended.

**Moore,** Charles Herbert. Born New York, New York, 1840; died Hartfield, Hampshire, England, 1930. Studied landscape painting in New York; exhibited for the first time at the National Academy of Design, New York, 1858. Established a studio at the Tenth Street Studio Building, New York, 1859–60. Exhibited at the Boston Athenaeum, 1861; National Academy of Design, New York, 1858–70. Appointed instructor in drawing and watercolor, Lawrence Scientific School, Harvard University, 1871; instructor in the principle of the fine arts, Harvard College, Cambridge, Massachusetts, 1874. Appointed assistant professor, 1891, and professor, 1896, at Harvard College. Appointed curator, Fogg Museum, Harvard University, 1895; director, 1896–1909. Retired to England, 1909;

devoted his remaining years to study of architecture. Influenced by writings of John Ruskin, with whom he studied in Italy, 1876–77; Moore was chief exponent of Ruskin's teachings in America.

**Moran,** Thomas. Born Bolton, Lancashire, England, 1837; died Santa Barbara, California, 1926. Emigrated with family to America, 1844; settled in Philadelphia. Apprenticed to wood engraving firm, 1852–55; opened a studio in Philadelphia with brother Edward. Exhibited watercolors, Pennsylvania Academy of the Fine Arts, 1856. Trip to London, 1861–62; studied works of Turner and Claude in National Gallery. Joined Hayden Expedition to Yellowstone Valley, 1871; Powell Expedition of Colorado River, 1873. Painting trip to Yosemite, California, 1876; Teton Mountains, Wyoming, 1879. Elected Academician, National Academy of Design, New York, 1884; established studio at East Hampton, Long Island, New York. Trips to Venice, Italy, 1886 and 1890. Painting trips to the Grand Canyon, Arizona, 1901, 1908, and 1910. Settled permanently in Santa Barbara, 1916.

**O'Keeffe,** Georgia. Born near Sun Prairie, Wisconsin, 1887. Decided to become an artist at age ten; attended Art Institute of Chicago, studied under John Vanderpoel, 1905–06. Studied at Art Students League, New York; pupil of William Merritt Chase, 1907–08. Gave up painting; worked as a commercial artist in Chicago, 1908–12. Began teaching art in public school, Amarillo, Texas, 1912. Taught at University of Virginia Art Department, summers 1913–16. First exhibition of drawings and watercolors, "291" Gallery, New York, 1916; first one-woman show there, 1917. Summer trip through Colorado and New Mexico; resumed teaching, Canyon, Texas, 1917. Established studio in New York; several summer trips to Lake George and Maine, 1918–28. Retrospective exhibition, The Brooklyn Museum, 1927. Summer trip to New Mexico; began frequent summer trips to Taos, 1929. Retrospective exhibitions, Art Institute of Chicago, 1943; Museum of Modern Art, New York, 1946. Began to live permanently at Abiquiu, New Mexico, 1949. Extensive travel in Europe, South America, and the Far East, 1953–69. Elected to American Academy of Arts and Letters, 1963; American Academy of Arts and Sciences, 1966. Presently working at Abiquiu.

**Peale,** Charles Willson. Born Queen Anne's County, Maryland, 1741; died Philadelphia, Pennsylvania, 1827. Worked in Annapolis, Maryland as saddler and woodcarver until about 1762. First lessons in painting from John Hesselius, Philadelphia. Trip to London, studied with Benjamin West, 1767–69. Returned to America; settled in Annapolis and began painting portraits, notably that

of George Washington, 1769–75. Settled permanently in Philadelphia after service with Continental Army, 1878. Opened first painting gallery in Philadelphia, 1782; established the Peale Museum in Independence Hall for display of natural history objects, 1786. With brother James, founded a family painting tradition; five of C. W. Peale's sons — Rembrandt, Raphaelle, Rubens, Franklin, and Titian Ramsay Peale — became well-known artists. Founding member of first artists' organization and art school in America, the Columbianum, 1795; founder of the Pennsylvania Academy of the Fine Arts, 1805.

**Peticolas,** Edward F. Born Pennsylvania, 1793; died Richmond, Virginia, about 1853. Brought to Richmond by parents, 1804; thought to have taken drawing lessons from Thomas Sully, about 1805. Traveled in Europe, visited England, France, and Italy, 1815–20. Returned to Virginia, 1820. Two further trips to Europe, 1824 and 1830–33. Gave up painting about 1845.

**Pleissner,** Ogden Minton. Born Brooklyn, New York, 1905. Studied at Art Students League; pupil of Frank Bridgman and Frank V. Du Mond. Worked on series of watercolors depicting war industries, 1942. Served as captain, U. S. Army Air Force, 1943; war artist-correspondent for *Life* magazine, 1944. Elected Associate, National Academy of Design, 1938; Academician, 1940. Served as Vice-President, National Academy of Design, 1949–50. Awarded Samuel F. B. Morse Medal of Honor, National Academy of Design, 1959; Altman Prize, 1961. Awarded Gold Medal, American Watercolor Society, 1956. Presently maintains studio in New York, New York.

**Potthast,** Edward Henry. Born Syracuse, New York, 1858; died New York, New York, 1916. Studied photography with his father and Ward V. Ranger, Syracuse; attended Syracuse University, 1873–75. Established studio in New York, New York, 1878; first works were watercolors influenced by the Barbizon School. Trip to Europe, early 1890s; studied at Académie Julian under J. P. Laurens and J. E. Blanc. Came under influence of Josef Israels and Anton Mauve. Returned to New York, 1888; moved to Connecticut where he painted on Fisher's Island, 1900. Established permanent summer studio at Noank, Connecticut after 1900. Autumn and winter in New York, taught at National Academy of Design; elected Academician, 1906.

**Prendergast,** Maurice Brazil. Born St. John's, Newfoundland, 1859; died New York, New York, 1924. Designed commercial posters in Boston, 1873. First trip to Europe, 1886; sketched in Wales and England. Sketching tours of New England, 1887–89; painted in Massachusetts and Maine. Second trip to Europe; studied at

Académies Julian and Colarossi under G. Courtois and J. L. Gérôme; Paris and summer painting trips to Normandy and Brittany, 1892–94. Returned to Boston to paint and open frame shop with brother Charles, 1894–97. Trip to Italy; painted in Venice, Siena, and Capri, 1898–99. Exhibited at Chase Gallery, Boston, and Art Institute of Chicago, 1900; Macbeth Gallery, New York, 1905. Exhibited in "The Eight" group show, Macbeth Gallery, New York, 1908. Returned to France; beginning of post-Impressionist influence, 1909–10. Works included in the Armory Show, New York, 1913. Moved permanently to New York, 1914; summer painting trips to New England, 1914–22. Memorial exhibition held at Cleveland Museum of Art, 1926.

**Richards,** William Trost. Born Philadelphia, Pennsylvania, 1833; died Newport, Rhode Island, 1905. Studied painting with Philadelphia artist Paul Weber, 1850; exhibited for the first time at Pennsylvania Academy of the Fine Arts, 1852. Trip to Europe, 1855 – 56; traveled to Paris, Lago Maggiore, Genoa, Pisa, and Florence. Brief trip to Düsseldorf, 1856; returned to Philadelphia. Elected Academician, Pennsylvania Academy of the Fine Arts, 1863. Summer painting trip to Mt. Desert, Maine, 1866. Second European trip, 1866–67; visited Germany, France, Switzerland, and Italy. Established permanent summer studio at Newport, Rhode Island, 1875; winter studio in Philadelphia. Frequent trips to England and the Continent, 1891–1905.

**Robinson,** Theodore. Born Irasburg, Vermont, 1852; died New York, New York, 1896. Studied at Art Students League, New York, 1874. Studied independently in Paris with C. Carolus-Duran and J. L. Gérôme, 1876 – 77. Exhibited at the Paris Salon of 1877. Traveled in France and Italy, 1878. Returned to New York, 1879; established studio, gave private lessons, and worked for John La Farge. Elected to Society of American Artists, 1881. Trip to France; painted in Paris, Barbizon, and Giverny, 1884–88. Became exponent of Impressionism under Monet's influence. Made annual trips to Europe, 1889–92. Worked winters in New York studio; summer painting trips to New England, New York, and New Jersey, 1893–95. Taught at Pennsylvania Academy of the Fine Arts; gave first one-man show at Macbeth Gallery, New York, 1895.

**Rothko,** Mark. Born Dvinsk, Russia, 1903; died New York, New York, 1970. Attended Yale University from 1921 to 1923. Studied drawing with Max Weber at the Art Students League in New York. His first exhibition was 1929, and in 1933 he had his first one – man show at the Contemporary Arts Gallery. In 1935 he co–founded The Ten, a group of artists who held annual shows for almost ten years. Throughout his career,

Rothko was also a teacher, holding positions at the Center Academy in Brooklyn, Brooklyn College, and Tulane University.

**Sargent,** John Singer. Born Florence, Italy, 1856; died London, England, 1925. Studied under C. Carolus-Duran, Paris, 1874 – 79; class included J. C. Beckwith, J. A. Weir, and Paul Helleu. Met Monet and began interest in impressionism; first trip to the United States, 1876. Began exhibiting at Paris Salon; won Honorable Mention, 1878. Painting trips to Morocco, Spain, Holland, and Italy, 1880. Painted in Venice, 1882. Exhibited *Madame X*, Paris Salon of 1884. Moved to London, 1885, began painting impressionist pictures during summers in Worcestershire, 1885 – 89. Painted portraits in the United States, in Newport, Boston, and New York, 1887 – 88 and 1890. Commissioned to paint mural decorations for Boston Public Library, 1890. Elected Associate, Royal Academy, London, 1894; Academician, National Academy of Design, New York, and Royal Academy, London, 1896. Embarked on a decade of prolific portrait painting in England and the United States, 1894–1904. Worked on mural decorations for Museum of Fine Arts, Boston, 1916–25.

**Schussele-Sommerville,** Christian. Born Guebviller, Alsace, France, 1824 or 1826; died Merchantville, New Jersey, 1879. Studied drawing and lithography at the Strasbourg Academy under M. Guérin, 1841. Worked as a chromolithographer, Paris; became a pupil of P. Delaroche, 1843 – 48. Emigrated to Philadelphia, became a lithographer, 1848. Drew designs for illustrations for periodicals and books, 1855-62; sketching trips to the South. Visited Europe, 1865–68; infirmities began to force him to abandon drawing. Offered a teaching position at Pennsylvania Academy of the Fine Arts, Philadelphia, 1870; chairman of drawing department until the end of his life. One of his pupils was Thomas Eakins.

**Shahn,** Ben. Born Kovno, Lithuania, 1898; died New York, New York, 1969. Emigrated with parents to the United States, 1906; settled in Brooklyn, New York. Employed as apprentice to commercial lithographer, 1913–17; continued to support himself as a lithographer until 1930. Attended New York University, City College of New York, 1918–22; National Academy of Design, 1922–25. Trips to Europe in 1925 and 1927–29; traveled in France, Italy, Spain, and North Africa, influenced by G. Rouault and R. Dufy. First exhibition of watercolors, Downtown Gallery, New York, 1930. Painted series of 23 gouaches, *Passion of Sacco and Vanzetti*, 1931–32. Assisted Diego Rivera on frescoes for Rockefeller Center, New York, 1933. Worked for WPA, Federal Art Project, 1938–39; painted series of frescoes for Bronx Post Office, New York. Fresco murals for Social

Security Building, Washington, D.C., 1940–42. Retrospective exhibition, Museum of Modern Art, New York, 1947. Began working on Hebraic themes, from 1948. Appointed to Charles Eliot Norton Chair of Poetics, Harvard University, 1956.

**Sheeler,** Charles. Born Philadelphia, Pennsylvania, 1883; died Irvington-on-Hudson, New York, 1965. Attended School of Industrial Art, Philadelphia, 1900–03; Pennsylvania Academy of the Fine Arts under William Merritt Chase, 1903 – 06. Summer painting trips with Chase; London and Holland in 1904, Spain in 1905. Turned to photography for livelihood, 1912. Exhibited six paintings in the Armory Show, New York, 1913. Moved studio from Philadelphia to New York, 1919; South Salem, New York in 1927; and Ridgefield, Connecticut in 1943. Retrospective exhibitions, Museum of Modern Art, New York, 1939; University of California, Los Angeles, 1954. A stroke forced him to stop painting, 1959. Received Award of Merit, American Academy of Arts and Letters, 1962.

**Sheets,** Millard Owen. Born Pomona, California, 1907. Studied at Chouinard Art Institute, Los Angeles, 1928; instructor at Chouinard, 1929 – 35, and University of Southern California, Los Angeles, 1934. Appointed professor of art, Scripps College, 1931. Worked as illustrator for *Life* magazine, Burma-India, 1943 – 44. Designed mural decorations for Detroit Public Library, Library of Notre Dame University, Catholic National Shrine, Washington, D. C., and Los Angeles City Hall. Worked in production design for Columbia Pictures, Hollywood, California, 1954 – 55. Elected Associate, National Academy of Design, New York, 1944. Presently lives at Gualala, California.

**Smith,** John Rubens. Born London, England, 1775; died New York, New York, 1849. Was taught drawing and mezzotint engraving by his father, John Raphael Smith; studied at Royal Academy, London and exhibited there from 1796 to 1811. First visit to America, 1802; emigrated to Boston, 1806. Opened a drawing academy in Boston, and resumed engraving and watercolor painting, 1806–09. Attempted to organize an art academy in Boston with assistance of Gilbert Stuart and Washington Allston, 1810. Moved to New York, 1816; returned to Boston, 1827, and published *Picturesque Anatomy*. Moved to Philadelphia, 1829; published a number of manuals for art instruction including *Art of Drawing the Human Figure*. Moved to New York, 1844; continued to give drawing instruction until his death.

**Thon,** William. Born New York, New York, 1906. Studied at Art Students League, New York, 1924 – 25. Awarded prize in Brooklyn Museum Biennial Exhibition of

American Watercolors, 1942; exhibited frequently in watercolor exhibitions at the Pennsylvania Academy of the Fine Arts beginning in 1950; National Academy of Design, New York, beginning in 1944. Elected Associate, National Academy of Design, 1949. Awarded fellowship, American Academy in Rome, 1947; grant from National Institute of Arts and Letters, 1951. Recipient of Doctor of Fine Arts, Bates College, Lewiston, Maine, 1957; Maine State Award, 1970. Presently lives at Port Clyde, Maine.

**Tobey,** Mark. Born Centerville, Wisconsin, 1890; died 1976, Basel, Switzerland. Worked as commercial artist while attending classes at Art Institute of Chicago, 1907. Trips to New York, 1911 – 17; studied briefly with Kenneth Hayes Miller and began working as portrait artist in charcoal. First one-man show, M. Knoedler & Co., New York, 1917. Moved to Seattle, Washington, 1923; began teaching and was introduced to Chinese brushwork. Trip to Europe, 1925 – 26; traveled in France, Spain, Greece, and Near East. Work included in exhibition of contemporary American art, Museum of Modern Art, New York, 1929. Trip to Europe and the Near East, 1932; to the Far East, 1934. First one-man exhibition, Seattle Art Museum, 1935; began first experiments with "white writing" style of painting. Painted mural decorations for W.P.A. Federal Art Project, Seattle, 1938. First one-man exhibition, Willard Gallery, New York, 1944; beginning of national reputation. Trip to Europe, 1955; traveled to Paris, Nice, and Basel, and gave first one-man show at Galerie Bucher, Paris. Elected to National Institute of Arts and Letters, 1956. Retrospective exhibitions, Musée des Arts Décoratifs, Paris, 1961; Museum of Modern Art, New York, 1962.

**Vanderlyn,** John. Born Kingston, New York, 1775; died Kingston, New York, 1852. Worked for a print seller in New York, while attending Archibald Robertson's Drawing Academy, 1792. Aaron Burr became his patron, sent him to Philadelphia to study with Gilbert Stuart, 1795 – 96; then to Paris to study under Antoine Vincent, 1796 – 1801. Returned to New York, established a studio, 1801 – 03. Moved to Paris, painted portraits and historical subjects, 1803 – 1815. Returned to New York, 1815; painted cyclorama of Versailles exhibited in City Hall Park. Commissioned by Congress to paint *Landing of Columbus* for Capitol, Washington, D.C., 1837. Returned to Paris to execute commission, 1842 – 44. Career ended in disappointment and obscurity; returned to Kingston where he died a pauper.

**Wall,** William Allen. Born New Bedford, Massachusetts, 1801; died New Bedford, Massachusetts, 1885. Worked as a watchmaker until 1828; turned to painting. Moved to New York, then to Philadelphia where he became a pupil of Thomas Sully. Trip to Europe, 1832–34; worked as copyist in art galleries in London and on the Continent. Returned to New Bedford, 1834; remained there for the rest of his life, painting views of the area.

**Wall,** William Guy. Born Dublin, Ireland, 1792; date and place of death unknown. Trained as an artist before his arrival in the United States in 1818; established a studio in New York. Painted views of the Hudson River and published them as *Hudson River Portfolio* between 1820 and 1828. Became a founder of the National Academy of Design, New York, 1826. Moved to Newport, Rhode Island, 1828 – 34. Lived in New Haven, Connecticut, 1834; Brooklyn, New York, 1836. Returned to Dublin, where he worked from 1836 until 1856. Returned to the United States, 1856; established studio at Newburgh, New York until 1862. Returned permanently to Ireland.

**Weber,** Max. Born Bialystok, Russia, 1881; died Great Neck, New York, 1961. Emigrated with parents to the United States, 1891; settled in Brooklyn, New York. Studied at Pratt Institute, 1898 – 1900; influenced by theories of design of Arthur W. Dow. Trip to Europe, 1905 – 08; became a close friend of Henri Rousseau and studied briefly with Henri Matisse. Exhibited at "291" Gallery, New York, 1909 and 1911. Painted in cubist manner, 1912 – 17. Refused invitation to exhibit in the Armory Show, 1913; one-man show, Newark Museum. Taught art appreciation at White School of Photography, New York, 1914 – 18; later at Art Students League, New York. Returned to figurative style, about 1920; turned to Hebraic themes and subjects dealing with social consciousness. Appointed honorary national chairman, American Artists' Congress, 1938–40.

**Weir,** Robert Walter. Born New York, New York, 1803; died New York, New York, 1889. Studied painting in New York while employed as a clerk, and became acquainted with the portrait painter John Wesley Jarvis. Attended American Academy of Art, New York, about 1820; studied anatomy at New York University Medical School and painted portraits. Trip to Italy, 1824 – 27; established a studio in Rome, shared rooms with sculptor Horatio Greenough. Returned to New York, 1827; established a studio there. Elected to National Academy of Design, 1829. Taught perspective drawing at National Academy School, 1832 – 34. Moved to West Point, New York, 1834; appointed instructor in drawing at U. S. Military Academy, later full professor. Held this post until retirement in 1876. Continued painting in New York; summer studio near Hoboken, New Jersey.

**Whistler,** James Abbott McNeill. Born Lowell, Massachusetts, 1834; died London, England, 1903. Dismissed after three years at U.S. Military Academy, West Point, 1854. Worked briefly as a cartographer for U.S. Coast and Geodetic Survey; learned drawing and etching. Departed the United States permanently, 1855; entered studio of C. G. Gleyre, Paris. Associated with the leaders of French modernism, including Courbet and Manet. Settled in London, 1859; began series of etchings, "Thames Set." Visited South America, 1866. First one-man exhibition, Flemish Gallery, London, 1874. Brought libel action against John Ruskin, 1878. Trip to Venice, 1880; worked on pastels and etchings. First large exhibition of watercolors, Dowdswell's Gallery, London, 1884; visited Holland and produced watercolors and etchings. Delivered "Ten O'Clock" lectures in London, Cambridge, and Oxford, 1885. Trip to France, 1888; made watercolors and etchings. Whistler's book *The Gentle Art of Making Enemies* published in London, 1890. Whistler's *Mother* bought for the Luxembourg Museum, Paris, 1891. Settled in Paris, 1893 – 95; painted portraits. Alternated residence between London and Paris, 1896–1903. Awarded grand prize for painting and engraving, Paris International Exposition, 1900.

**Whittredge,** (Thomas) Worthington. Born near Springfield, Ohio, 1820; died Summit, New Jersey, 1910. Employed as house painter, Cincinnati, Ohio, about 1837; worked also as sign painter and made daguerreotypes. Began portrait painting, about 1840. A Cincinnati patron paid for a trip to Europe, 1849; settled in Düsseldorf and studied at the Academy. Settled in Rome, 1854 – 59. Returned to the United States, 1859; took a studio in the Tenth Street Building, New York. Elected to National Academy of Design, 1861; served as president of the Academy, 1874 – 77. Presumed to have accompanied the Pope Expedition to the West, 1866; trip to the Rocky Mountains with J. F. Kensett and S. R. Gifford, 1870. Moved studio to Summit, New Jersey, 1880. Trips to Mexico in 1893 and 1896. His *Autobiography* published in 1905, a primary source of information about the history of the Hudson River School.

**Whorf,** John. Born Winthrop, Massachusetts, 1903; died Provincetown, Massachusetts, 1959. Studied at Boston Museum of Fine Arts School, with Max Bohm, 1920 – 23; summers with Charles Hawthorne's school, Provincetown, Massachusetts. First exhibition of watercolors, Hartford, Connecticut, 1923. Studied at the École des Beaux-Arts, Paris; Académie Grand Chaumiere, late 1920s. Painting trips to Canada and West Indies, 1930 – 38. Awarded honorary degree, Master of Arts,

Harvard University, 1938. Elected Associate, National Academy of Design, New York, 1947.

**Wood,** Thomas Waterman. Born Montpelier, Vermont, 1828; died New York, New York, 1903. Self-taught in oil painting; first professional lessons from Chester Harding, Boston, 1846–47. Became itinerant portrait painter, 1847–58; visited Quebec, Canada, New York, Washington, D.C., and Baltimore. Trip to Europe, 1858–60; worked as copyist in galleries in London, Paris, Florence, and Rome. Returned to the United States, 1860; worked for a period in Louisville, Kentucky and Nashville, Tennessee and developed interest in genre painting. Established a studio in New York, 1867. Elected Academician, National Academy of Design, New York, 1871; president of the National Academy, 1891–99. Served as president, American Water Color Society, 1878–87. Founder, New York Etching Club, 1878. Established an art gallery for display of his own works and a collection of European paintings, Montpelier, 1895.

**Woodville,** Richard Caton. Born Baltimore, Maryland, 1825; died, London, England, 1855. Wanted a career in medicine; enrolled in University of Maryland, 1842. Decided to become a painter sometime before 1845. Exhibited a painting at the National Academy of Design, New York, 1845. Trip to Europe, 1845; settled in Düsseldorf, studied genre painting with Carl Ferdinand Sohn. Worked in Düsseldorf until 1851; frequent exhibitor at National Academy of Design, New York. After 1851, lived in Paris and London; supported by his patron Robert Gilmor of Baltimore.

**Wyeth,** Andrew Newell. Born Chadd's Ford, Pennsylvania, 1917. Studied under his father, N. C. Wyeth. First exhibition, Philadelphia Art Alliance, 1936; first one-man exhibition, Macbeth Gallery, New York, 1937. Began annual summer residence at Cushing, Maine; winter studio at Chadd's Ford. Invited to exhibit at International Watercolor Exhibition, Art Institute of Chicago, 1941. Given Award of Merit, American Academy of Arts and Letters, 1947; elected to membership in the Academy in 1956. First major retrospective exhibition, Currier Gallery of Art, Manchester, New Hampshire, 1951. Elected Academician, National Academy of Design, 1945; awarded first prize in watercolor, National Academy, 1946. Awarded gold medal of honor, Pennsylvania Academy of the Fine Arts, Philadelphia, 1966; retrospective exhibition. One-man exhibition, The White House, Washington, D.C., 1970; first artist ever to be so honored.

**Zorach,** William. Born Euberick-Kovno, Lithuania, 1887; died Brooklyn, New York, 1966. Emigrated with family to the United States, 1893; settled at Port Clinton, Ohio, 1893–96. Family moved to Cleveland, Ohio; worked as commercial lithographer, 1902–08. Studied drawing and painting with Henry Keller, Cleveland School of Art. Studied at National Academy of Design, New York, 1908–10; summers as lithographer, Cleveland. Trip to Europe, 1910; studied with J. E. Blance, Paris. Exhibited at Salon a l'Automne, Paris, 1911; the Armory Show, New York, 1913. Began working in sculpture, 1917; by 1922, gave up painting in oils but continued to work in watercolors. First one-man exhibition, Daniel Gallery, New York, 1915; represented in Pan Pacific International Exposition, San Francisco. Appointed instructor, Art Students League, New York, 1929. Sculpture commissioned for Radio City Music Hall, New York, 1932.

# BIBLIOGRAPHY

Arnason, H.H. *History of Modern Art.* New York: Harry Abrams, 1976.

Baur, John I.H. *Revolution and Tradition in Modern American Art.* Cambridge: Harvard University Press, 1951.

Brown, Milton. *American Painting from the Armory Show to the Depression.* Princeton: Princeton University Press, 1970.

Callow, James. *Kindred Spirits: Knickerbocker Writers and American Artists, 1807-1855.* Chapel Hill: University of North Carolina Press, 1967.

Cheney, M.S.C. *Modern Art in America.* New York: McGraw, 1939.

Clement, Clara E., and Hutton, Laurence. *Artists of the Nineteenth Century and Their Work.* Repro. of 1894 ed. New York: Arno Press.

Cowdrey, Bartlett, ed. *National Academy of Design Exhibition Record, 1826-1860.* 2 vols. New York, 1943.

Doerner, Max. *Materials of the Artist.* New York: Harcourt-Brace, 1949.

Dunlap, William. *A History of the Rise and Progress of the Arts of Design in the United States.* Revised ed., 3 vols., New York: Arno Press, 1964.

Flexner, James Thomas. *That Wilder Image: The Painting of America's Native School from Thomas Cole to Winslow Homer.* New York: Dover, 1970.

Frankenstein, Alfred. *After the Hunt.* Berkeley: University of California Press, 1975.

Gallatin, Albert E. *American Watercolorists.* New York: Dutton, 1922.

Gardner, Albert Ten Eyck. *History of Watercolor Painting in America.* New York: Reinhold, 1966.

Groce, George C., and Wallace, David H. *The New-York Historical Society's Dictionary of Artists in America, 1564-1860.* New Haven: Yale University Press, 1957.

Hardie, Martin. *Water-Colour Painting in Britain: The Eighteenth Century.* New York: Barnes and Noble, 1966, London: B.T. Batsford, Ltd.

Hoopes, Donelson F. *Eakins Watercolors.* New York: Watson-Guptill, 1971.

——*Sargent Watercolors.* New York: Watson-Guptill, 1970.

——*Winslow Homer Watercolors.* New York: Watson-Guptill, 1969.

Kootz, Samuel M. *Modern American Painters.* New York: Harcourt, 1930.

Larkin, Oliver W. *Art and Life in America.* Revised ed. New York: Holt, Rinehart, Winston, 1960.

Mayer, Ralph. *The Artist's Handbook of Materials and Techniques.* 3rd Revised ed. New York: Viking Press, 1970.

*M. and M. Karolik Collection of American Paintings: 1815-1865.* Boston: Museum of Fine Arts, 1949.

*M. and M. Karolik Collection of American Water Colors and Drawings, 1800-1875.* 2 vols. Boston: Museum of Fine Arts, 1962.

Novak, Barbara. *American Painting of the Nineteenth Century.* New York: Praeger, 1969.

Reynolds, Graham. *Concise History of Watercolor.* New York: Transatlantic, 1974.

Richardson, Edgar P. *American Romantic Painting.* New York: Weyhe, 1944.

——*Painting in America.* revised ed. New York: Crowell, 1965.

Stokes, I.N. Phelps. *The Iconography of Manhattan Island.* 6 vols. New York: R.H. Dodd, 1915-1928.

Tuckerman, Henry T. *Book of the Artists.* New York: G.P. Putnam & Sons, 1867.

Warren, Henry. *Painting in Water Colors.* New York, 1856.

Williams, Hermann Warner, Jr. *Mirror to the American Past: A Survey of American Genre Painting, 1750-1900.* Boston: New York Graphic Society, 1973.

# INDEX

*(Note: Paintings appear on pages numbered in italics.)*